The Whole Child

The Whole Child

Restoring Wonder to the Art of Parenting

Seamus Carey

ROWMAN & LITTLEFIELD PUBLISHERS, INC.
Lanham • Boulder • New York • Oxford

ROWMAN & LITTLEFIELD PUBLISHERS, INC.

Published in the United States of America
by Rowman & Littlefield Publishers, Inc.
A Member of the Rowman & Littlefield Publishing Group
4501 Forbes Boulevard, Suite 200, Lanham, Maryland 20706
www.rowmanlittlefield.com

PO Box 317
Oxford
OX2 9RU, UK

British Library Cataloguing in Publication Information Available

Library of Congress Cataloging-in-Publication Data
Carey, Seamus, 1965–
    The whole child : restoring wonder to the art of parenting / Seamus Carey.
        p.   cm.
    Includes bibliographical references and index.
    ISBN 0-7425-1486-2 (hardcover : alk. paper)—ISBN 0-7425-1487-0 (pbk. : alk. paper)
    1. Parents—Attitudes. 2. Perspective (Philosophy) 3. Wisdom. 4. Wonder. 5. Parent and child. I. Title: Restoring wonder to the art of parenting. II. Title.
    HQ755.83.C37 2003
    649'.1—dc21   2003000724

Printed in the United States of America

For
my wife,
Noreen,
and our children,
Caitriona, Anna, and James

Contents

~

Preface

While driving home on the New Jersey Turnpike one night after teaching an ethics seminar, I found myself rehashing in my head the discussion that had taken place in class an hour before. Over the previous weeks, our class discussions had been more lively than usual. The students seemed very interested in understanding the details of Aristotle's *Ethics*, and I was trying to accommodate them by making his thought as relevant to their lives as I could. Since it was a night class, many of the students were older and working full-time jobs. Some had children, and there were even a couple of grandparents in the class. Since the traditional college-age students in the class were going through the process of separating from their parents, the parent–child relationship was something we all had in common. It proved to be a fertile topic for discussing the ethical theories we were trying to understand.

Parenting is particularly important to me. At the time I was teaching that class I had two young daughters, and we were expecting a third child, who turned out to be our first son. As I prepared to talk about texts that I had read numerous times before, they came to life with a new freshness as I reflected on their relevance to parenting. In fact, the relationship between philosophy and parenting took such a firm hold of my mind that I could scarcely think of anything else. It seemed to me that there was a great deal of wisdom that could be mined from philosophers throughout the ages to provide desperately needed insight into parenting and the development of children. This notion was driven home at the end of one of our class discussions when the grandmother in the class, with a look that combined awe and resignation, said to nobody in particular: "Aristotle just made me realize everything that I have done wrong with my children for so many years."

This was a serious and intelligent woman who, like so many parents, never had access to the insights of the great philosophers. She never knew of the importance of wonder as a way to supplement ordinary ways of thinking. She never thought of listening as a skill that needed to be developed rather than just a biological fact. She was never exposed to the ontology of Being, and the role of human beings in that ontology. As a result, she had accepted her understanding of her children and how she would deal with them from her parents and from society at large uncritically. I felt for her as she sat there with much of her life passing before her eyes. As I reflected on her comment on my ride home, I was moved to explore these ideas in greater depth. These ideas so dramatically shaped my life and my relationship with my family, I was compelled to share them with others.

I thought of all of this before I reached the George Washington Bridge to cross the Hudson into New York. I was so excited by the idea that I stopped at an Irish café in the Bronx to write down my thoughts. I ordered a pint of Guinness and let my thoughts and my pint settle together. I needed to find a coherent perspective from which my ideas could begin to make sense, a general theme that could be developed from these different thoughts that had me under siege. To begin this sorting process, I turned my thoughts to the philosophers and the ideas that have had the most influence on me. One of those thinkers is Martin Heidegger, a twentieth-century German thinker. One of the central themes of Heidegger's work that transformed my understanding of how people relate to the world and to each other is *das Heilen*, which is translated as "the hale." Heidegger uses this term to connote the wholeness, wholesomeness, and holiness of human life that results when we relate to the event of Being (to reality in general and the reality of others) with a mature, open-minded, and highly perceptive disposition. The hale, I thought, is what we want to nurture in our children and in our relationships with them.

As a parent, I would be pleased if my children developed a personality or character that could be described as wholesome and holy. In fact, these are qualities that almost all parents want to cultivate in their children. The best ideas of philosophers throughout the ages reveal, in different and creative ways, the wholesome and holy potential of human life. If philosophy could provide parents with some insight and perspective on the meaning and methods of cultivating the whole child, families and society in general would benefit. The overarching goal of *The Whole Child* then is to make philosophical wisdom and insight into wholesomeness and Being relevant to and useful in the nurturing and guidance of children.

After deciding on the general theme, I thought about the most effective way to present these ideas. One of the downfalls of philosophical discourse is that it is often inaccessible to nonphilosophers. As a result, philosophy tends to be limited to the academy, in which philosophers communicate in languages so specialized that they have a hard time understanding even themselves. Such language would be of little benefit to parents who are so busy in their daily lives that they are lucky to find time to read a book, much less one that is barely comprehensible. To avoid this problem, I have tried to the best of my ability to present important philosophical ideas in such a way that anyone interested can understand and enjoy them. I have relied on stories from my own experiences as a parent as well as observations from literature, popular culture, and the everyday world to introduce these ideas. By combining these stories with philosophical commentaries, I hope to offer parents new perspectives from which to relate to their children. These new perspectives will include healthier, more rewarding expectations of children and parents while also pointing toward new paths by which such expectations can be achieved.

In line with making this book both thought provoking and enjoyable, its structure playfully follows the sequence of letters in the title. The title of each chapter begins with a sequential letter in the title *Whole Child* (with the exception of the letters "H" and "L" in Child, since these occur twice in the title). I have combined these letters in the title of the final chapter, "Higher Love." This strategy occurred to me when I realized that "W," the first letter in the title, is also the first letter in "Wisdom and Wonder." Philosophy (*philo-sophia*) literally means love of wisdom. The philosophical experience in the pursuit of wisdom begins with an experience of wonder; hence the title of the first chapter, "The Wisdom of Wonder." From this first association of letters, almost every other chapter fell into place immediately. As a result, the book consists of nine chapters, which can be read as a series of independent essays or in the traditional sequential fashion. Either approach should help the reader find some new ways to think about his or her relationship to children and about human nature in general.

Acknowledgments

There are a number of people who have played an important role in the formation of this book. I want to thank James Mustich, Fernand Beck, Michael Carey, Kate Curnin, and Kevin Curnin for their invaluable comments and support during the early stages of this work. Sara Wolford, the director of the Early Childhood Center at Sarah Lawrence College, generously took the time to read early drafts of the text while running one of the finest schools in the country. I am also grateful to the teachers at the Early Childhood Center, especially Sonna Schupak, Marcia Levy, and Susan Schwimmer, who demonstrate the true potential of teaching and education. Shannon Duval made excellent suggestions, all of which led to improvements in the text. During the final stages of writing, Bill Buse posed specific challenges that forced me to refine the book more than I thought I could.

Not only would I not have attempted to write a book like this, I would most likely not be doing philosophy if not for the encouragement and support that Roger Gottlieb has provided over the past five years. His work as a philosopher and as a parent keeps me humble. I also want to thank Amelio D'Onofrio, whose influence is deeply felt in each chapter. His insight and references, in particular to works of psychology, have made this a much better book than it would have been otherwise. Finally, I want to thank my parents for the wisdom and love they bring to the art of parenting.

~

Nurturing the Hidden Depths of Children

Under the circumstances, the four-hour bus ride my wife and four-year-old daughter took from Manhattan to the Bronx at noon on September 11, 2001, was nothing to complain about. The bus was full of people as well as tension, fear, and at times hysteria. My daughter was the only child on the bus, and, according to my wife, she provided adults who were sitting nearby some relief from their anxiety. Perhaps they found some comfort in her four-year-old innocence, because they knew that innocence was something that had just been lost in the tragedy that was unfolding behind them. Stories of devastation were circulating around the bus. Passengers were frantically calling on cell phones, checking in with family and friends. Some couldn't get through and for them the anxiety grew. Those who did manage to talk with someone heard stories of incomprehensible horror.

While my daughter talked with strangers on the bus, telling them about her school and her friends, she also listened attentively to what was transpiring around her. She heard descriptions of buildings collapsing and witnessed adults crying. She understood that traffic was causing the bus to move slowly. But there were many things she did not understand, and so she asked my wife. She wanted to know why people would try to hurt other people by crashing a plane into a building. She wanted to know if her uncle, who is a firefighter and was involved in the rescue, was safe. She wanted to know if her teacher, Marcia, had been hurt. When my wife asked her why she was concerned about Marcia, she told her that Marcia is Jewish and the people who crashed the planes don't like Jewish people.

1

Children are incredibly perceptive, sensitive, and thoughtful. They focus on distinctive details of events that adults often fail to recognize. Their sensitivity leads them to feel the impact of details that adults manage to deflect, ignore, or minimize. They will take weeks, months, and years to think about and process the meaning of events. We are often astonished to hear a child passionately articulate his or her thoughts and feelings about events that we have long forgotten. Parents and children often perceive different worlds through the same events. As a result, it is easy to forget that children are affected by events in ways that we often do not recognize or understand. This became evident to us in the days following the terror attacks, as our daughter began to express subtle but unmistakable concern and anxiety.

Like so many New Yorkers, we knew people who were killed on September 11. In the days that followed, watching the news or reading the paper was an emotional experience. My wife and I knew how sad we felt. What we didn't realize early on was how much these events had affected our daughter. We did not try to hide things from her. That would have been impossible, since she had been in Manhattan when the attacks occurred, and she could see that the event was affecting us. We did try to minimize her exposure to the stories that followed on the news. This wasn't too hard, since she always walked out of the room when I turned on the nightly news anyhow. The night after the attack, however, as I sat down to watch the news, rather than leaving the room, my daughter dropped what she was doing and ran into the room to turn off the television. She began to cry as she tried to tell me that she didn't want to hear about the people getting hurt anymore. She had seen and heard enough suffering.

At that moment, I was reminded once again, as I have been repeatedly since my first niece was born twelve years ago, just how sensitive and perceptive children are. While Caitriona did not speak about the tragedy for almost two days after the bus ride home, she was processing everything that was going on around her. What we observed in her behavior was merely a veil hiding her sorrow and fear. For a short while, in the days that followed, she became fearful of the dark and of ordinary household noises. Like all of us, she was feeling a heightened sense of anxiety in her daily life. Like us, she needed reassurance about her safety to overcome that anxiety.

As parents, we are faced with the responsibility of helping our children achieve their full potential as mature, well-rounded citizens. The story of my daughter's response to the terror attacks is but one example of the perceptual and emotional depth of children. As they develop from infancy to adolescence and young adulthood, this depth of feeling and perception grows, as does their emotional, psychological, and spiritual needs. As parents, we need to gain as much insight and understanding as possible into the background experiences of our children, because it is there, below the surface, that their most intense feelings and most essential needs lie. It is out of the interplay between the surface expressions of our children and their hidden worlds of feeling and emotion that the whole child develops. Parents must try to understand this interplay and relate to it if they are to be successful in nurturing the whole child. Philosophers throughout the ages, and more recently psychologists, have illuminated the dynamics of this interplay for us. *The Whole Child* is intended to share some of that light to assist parents and children in developing their whole and highest selves.

Some of this book was written before September 11, 2001, and some was written after. Nobody can say with any certainty how deep and wide the impact of that tragic day in our history will be. One thing is sure: The destruction at the World Trade Center and the Pentagon will change life in the United States for a long time. Shortly after that day, New York City was scrambling to return to what many people were calling "normalcy." What commentators were referring to as normalcy, as far as I could tell, was an attempt to recapture the routines that had defined their lives before the tragedy. They were longing to get back into their offices and perhaps, more importantly, into the mind-sets that define who they are in the daily routines of everyday life.

Returning to one's daily routine is probably a necessary part of the healing process following such a tragedy. But it can only be a part. The emotional and psychological impact of such an event cannot be underestimated. This is true for people of all ages and all walks of life. This event had a numbing effect on almost everyone. Some were unusually quiet and too emotional to speak. Others expressed sadness, hurt, anger, and confusion. Trauma affects different people in different ways. To return to the routines of everyday life, however, is a part of the healing process only if we are attentive to the psychological and emotional undercurrents that are stirring below the everyday mind-set of "normalcy." If we try to push such an event behind us too fast, the emotional and psychological undercurrents may reemerge in unrecognizable and possibly destructive forms at a later time.

I draw on the events of September 11 and what followed as a dramatic example of the constant challenge we face to integrate the unconscious dimensions of the psyche into everyday life. As parents, we must be attentive to the unconscious life of our children, but it is equally important to nurture an awareness and integration of our own hidden selves. Without this integration, it becomes difficult, if not impossible, to guide our children with the direction and conviction they need.

One thing that dramatic or traumatic events can do for us is force us to reflect on the fundamental questions of human life and our relationships with others. Such events are interruptions that call into question many of the principles and ideas of living that we often take for granted. One of the perennial tragedies of human life is that we often wait until a major tragedy occurs before clarifying and pursuing our highest priorities. One of the primary tasks of philosophy is to help us gain some insight and wisdom to identify and address the most important issues of human life on our own terms, before tragic interruptions and before it is too late to act on our wisdom.

It is widely known, but too often forgotten, that children first learn how to understand and respond to the world by watching and imitating adults they respect. They learn how to feel about themselves through the responses their presence and actions generate in others, especially their parents. They harbor deeply felt emotions and needs beneath the surface of everyday consciousness, which parents must try to understand and carry forth in a respectful and nurturing way. Philosophy is most effective in sharpening and sustaining our sensitivity to the hidden emotions and needs of both children and adults. Making the effort to encounter these hidden depths means we do not have to wait for major interruptions or tragedies to do it for us. This book, then, is an account of the dynamics involved in sustaining an awareness of the emotional, psychological, and spiritual development of children that is necessary to realize their highest potential.

Whole, Not Total

The potential and the happiness of children cannot be quantified or measured. As parents, therefore, we must be vigilant in caring for and nurturing all parts of their lives. In doing so, it is important to distinguish between the concepts *whole* and *total*. The *whole* is intended to convey the wholesome and holy dimensions of human experience, which are found by uncovering what is hidden and mysterious about human beings. These parts of our experience defy complete or total conceptualization or quantification. *Totality*, on the other hand, implies completeness or the possibility that something can be completed or finished. If all of the parts are present, we have a totality. If there is a totality, we can quantify and measure.

The whole that we are referring to is not static. It is something that is never complete or finished. It is always on the way, transforming itself and being transformed. It is constantly evolving into something it is not yet. In speaking of wholeness, therefore, we are not taking inventory of something that already exists in full. Rather, we are uncovering those organic dimensions of the child and our relationships with children that often go unnoticed and uncultivated. There is always more to children and more to our relationships with them than we are aware of. The philosophical task is to cultivate and sustain a vigilantly open mind that is attentive to the hidden and changing depths of children and of our own lives.

In thinking through the idea of the "whole child," we must resist the idea of totality, because human existence is bound up in numerous relationships that influence who we are and who we can become. According to Heidegger, our most important task is to get our relationship with Being in order. As long our relationship to the fundamental reality of the cosmos is askew, we can never develop into the people we are meant to be. Just as our lives are always in the process of becoming something new, reality itself is emerging and evolving. As free and creative beings, we participate in and contribute to that evolution. We interact with Being, or reality, on many different levels. These interactions hold the potential to appropriate the infinite energy of Being in the most efficient ways. But such appropriation requires us to understand the nature of Being and the nature of the individual beings that we encounter in our daily lives. As we will examine in chapter 1, in our discussion of wonder, it is often necessary to alter our basic disposition toward others from one that seeks to measure, control, and manipulate to one that seeks to understand by welcoming that which is constantly revealing something new to us. This shift in attitude is central to ontology, or the study of Being, which we will explore in chapter 3. For now it is sufficient to point out that the nature of Being as something that is evolving and never fully present at any moment also applies to the being of children. They are never fully present to us. Therefore, if we are to be facilitators of the healthy development of the whole child, we must recognize the need for constant vigilance in listening for the hidden voices that come from the depths of the child's being.

Art, Not Technique

The subtitle of the book refers to the *art* of parenting. This is not one of the "how-to" books that fill the shelves of bookstores today. It does not provide menus or techniques to follow in disciplining a child or in alleviating rivalry between siblings. It does not provide steps to take to get your child to eat dinner. While there are many useful "how-to" books, parents who have consulted these books, as I have, realize that they have limited relevance to the specific needs of their families. The premise of "how-to" parenting books is that parenting is a *techne*. That is, they assume that there are techniques that, if mastered, will lead to successful parenting. But children are far too complex to fit into categories or respond predictably to prescribed techniques. When the technique reaches its effective limit or breaks down, we are left to our own resources to figure out the next move. In other words, we must think for ourselves. So *The Whole Child* is not a fixed approach to anticipated events, but pursues fluid understanding of the evolving act of parenthood. Beyond techniques, a philosophical grounding will help parents better understand parenting, better understand the universal dynamics of the parent–child relationship, and therefore be better prepared to deal with any situation.

This is not to say that parents do not benefit from intelligent techniques. But techniques without the more basic understanding of the nature and needs of children and the role of parents are doomed to failure. Just as someone who has never played the piano cannot simply follow a manual and successfully play music, a parent cannot follow prescribed techniques and nurture a healthy, well-adjusted child. While an artist may follow techniques to learn a movement or a skill, she is an artist because that skill becomes a part of a deep understanding of her abilities and of the material with which she works. Likewise, any technique that a parent may use must be a part of a mature, insightful, and understanding disposition if it is to be effective. *The Whole Child* is intended to help parents uncover a thoughtful context within which they can understand the essential needs of their children and provide insightful guidance that will facilitate the healthy development of all aspects of their children's lives.

The Whole Child also intends to help parents uncover and nurture those parts of their own lives that the demands of everyday life usually force us to forget. In fact, the activity of philosophy is sometimes described as a process of remembering. What does philosophy help us to remember? Some argue that the primary purpose of philosophy is to help us to remember the inner self.[1] That is, philosophy helps us to remember that part of the self that is concerned with the questions of ultimate meaning in life; questions such as "Who am I?" and "What is my purpose in life?" In remembering the part of the self that asks questions of ultimate concern, we remember or reattune ourselves to a dimension of experience that is obliterated by the fast pace of twenty-first-century life. This is the ontological dimension of existence, a dimension in which all of our everyday activities, such as work, play, and caring for children, find their deepest meaning. By uncovering this dimension of our lives we gain access to the deep wisdom that has been accumulating, not only throughout our own individual lives since birth, but also throughout billions of years of evolution. This wisdom is carried forth subtly and often imperceptibly in the memory of our cells. In order to access this dimension of unconscious, embodied wisdom and meaning we need to cultivate our ability to perceive its hidden and often mysterious qualities. Such cultivation and development enables us to see and appreciate a vast universe in every being, the universe in which we participate, and of which we have the privilege of being conscious.

The philosophical process of remembering begins with self-examination. It forces us to take account of the values or ideals that we hold to be true and good and the habits by which we live. For most of us, there is dissonance between our ideals and our habits. We form habits beginning in infancy and they often remain unconscious. As we mature and reflect on the habits we have formed, we find that they sometimes conflict with the ideals we hold to be true and good. Self-reflection is necessary to identify areas of dissonance in our lives and to work toward bridging the space between ideals and habits.

This process of self-reflection is an essential part of good parenting. Parents who fail to examine their own lives often engage in what psychoanalyst Alice Miller calls "cycles of contempt." As long as parents are unaware of the patterns of behavior that have been forming in their unconscious since early childhood, they often deflect deeply repressed pain away from themselves and onto their children. So while parents often want what is best for their children, their unconscious fears and unresolved pain often prevent them from providing the nurturing guidance that children need to reach their potential. Philosophical self-examination can begin the process of overcoming such hurtful patterns of behavior by bringing parents into the light of conscious awareness.

Philosophy, the process of self-examination and remembrance, is an ongoing task. It is a challenging task insofar as it forces one to face up to the hidden and hurtful parts of the soul. But as parents become more comfortable with this process, they will begin to cultivate a firm, but flexible, equanimity from which they can relate intelligently and effectively with their children. Through serious philosophical reflection, parents will find the psychological and emotional space that is often so hard to procure within the congestion of daily household life. For parents who spend most of their time with children, this space is precious. When parents work from this inner space and inner equanimity, the techniques that they employ can evolve into an art form. One of the joys of reading an effective book is that one need not make a physical journey to find such freedom and space. The mind and the imagination can be equally, if not more, effective in doing so.

By engaging in serious self-reflection and deepening their understanding of the nature of children through philosophy, working parents can make the transition from the thought processes and emotions of professional life to the role of parenting much easier. Time with children will be spent more meaningfully if the superficial and nonproductive aspects of the relationship are removed through philosophical reflection. Such reflection will help working parents sort through the many pressing issues they face on a daily basis. The intensity of these issues often makes it difficult to leave them outside of the home. *The Whole Child* can help parents to do just that by uncovering different levels of awareness from which they can think about and relate to their children. It can facilitate a more intimate, rewarding, and effective relationship between parents and their children.

Psychology and Philosophy

Along with "how-to" parenting books, there are numerous books that address the development of children and the role of parents from a psychological perspective. I have always found the most important psychologists to be heavily influenced by philosophy and legitimate philosophers in their own right. *The Whole Child* recognizes and draws extensively on works on the psychology of child development. In doing so, it extends the complementary relationship between psychology and philosophy. It develops the insights of twentieth-century psychology by initiating a conversation among thinkers such as Donald Winnicott, Erik Erikson, Alice Miller, and Robert Coles and philosophers from Plato to Heidegger. Placing these thinkers in conversation with one another, *The Whole Child* is a philosophical work informed by psychology. However, it differs from psychological works in at least two important ways.

First, it is widely known that theories of psychology are born out of their philosophical predecessors over the past two and a half millennia. There is little in theories of psychology that has not been addressed in some form by philosophy. But psychology has provided important research and data to give these theories more direct relevance to human behavior and human dysfunction. By placing the insights of twentieth-century psychology in a deep and rich philosophical background, we can provide a deep, broad, and meaningful context for parents to understand the nature and essential needs of their children.

Second, one of the biggest challenges that parents face in raising their children is to remain cognizant of the highest goals in human life. It is often the case that we lose sight of these goals under the pressure of competing and surviving in the fast-paced world of the twenty-first century. By reflecting on philosophical wisdom, both ancient and contemporary, we bring our highest goals and the values required to achieve them back into focus. We recall that which is most important to living a good life. We remember that human beings have the ability to achieve ever-higher levels of awareness. Those who achieve higher awareness are more likely to live a fulfilling life themselves and thereby model positive behavior for their children. *The Whole Child* hopes to contribute to the higher awareness of its readers so that they can better enjoy and cultivate the magic of their children, and so that their children can better enjoy and contribute to the magic of the world.

Notes

1. Jacob Needleman, *The Heart of Philosophy* (New York: Harper, 1986).

PART I

~

PARENTAL WISDOM

CHAPTER ONE

The Wisdom of Wonder

At the edge of the vegetable garden at the back of my in-laws' house there are two large wooden beams, approximately ten feet long and eight inches square, stacked on top of each other. These beams supported the entire house before they were removed in a renovation a number of years ago. I sat beside these massive pieces of wood on a recent sunny spring afternoon and noticed that they were now serving as the homestead for a colony of carpenter ants. At first I took little notice of these tiny creatures, but after a while I began to notice patterns in their movements. At regular intervals of approximately three or four seconds, two or three ants emerged from between the two beams and dropped what they had wrestled from the inner beam down to the concrete wall on which the beams were resting. At the corner of the beam, where it met the concrete, there was a small pile of wood moss that the ants had dropped from above. As I admired the fruits of their labor, I noticed another group of approximately four ants working on that pile, taking what had fallen from above to the edge of the concrete wall and dropping it down another level, twelve inches below. These tiny creatures, which we usually think nothing of squashing under a dirty sneaker, had a system to get their work done efficiently. Somehow, they understood, and dutifully performed, their roles as members of a community.

A sense of wonder came over me as I thought of the ancient lineage of these ants and watched them cooperate with such determination and grace. They were guided by an evolutionary wisdom that their species developed over thousands of years as a means of survival. This cooperative wisdom is now instinct for them, as natural as breathing or eating. As I contemplated, I was transported out of the hours and minutes of this particular Saturday and into a place without time. I was in the middle of a genuine experience of wonder.

Some time later my father-in-law came to sit beside me and I pointed out the source of my amazement. As I was explaining the working patterns of the ants, he reminded me that the house was for sale. Wonder quickly turned to concern when we realized that the seven or eight working ants that I was admiring were not alone. They were working for others hidden away between the two giant beams. If a colony of carpenter ants got across the backyard and into the house, they would dissect the beams and studs of the house in the same way they were dissecting these beams. We had to do something, so we moved the top beam off the bottom beam to see what was taking place between them. The timelessness of wonder quickly vanished under the weight of practicality.

Moving the top beam had an effect similar to that of parents coming home early from vacation to find their children throwing a party for the neighborhood; the ants scattered as quickly as they could in every direction. This was not surprising. Ants, like all living creatures, have survival instincts. As I looked more closely at this chaotic flight for safety, I saw dozens of small, white, ball-like figures among the frantic ants. I also noticed that some of the ants were not going directly for the edge of the beam to get away, but were doubling back to pick up their eggs. For a brief moment, I fell back into a sense of awe and wonder as I watched the ants stumble and struggle awkwardly to get away with the eggs perched between their front legs. The ants not only had an instinct to survive, they also had an instinct to protect their young.

The experience of wonder initiated for me by the ants is something that many parents experience by watching their children. Imagine the wonder of a parent witnessing a child's first steps, or first words; or watching his child recite a poem or a piece of music before an audience for the first time. Such accomplishments, which are infinitely more complex and personal than the instinctual responses of a colony of ants, can transport a parent out of the monotony of everyday demands and stresses and into the deep well of the meaning and emotion that color a healthy relationship between parents and children. But too often in our world, parents miss these experiences, because for too long they have neglected the human need and capacity for wonder. Practicality supplants all else, eclipsing our ability to wonder. When this occurs, the necessary tension between wonder and practicality, between possibility and necessity, is lost. In losing this tension parents also lose the possibility for a healthy perspective from which to cultivate the vision and the disposition they need to effectively guide and nurture their children.

A week after having been treated to the experience of wonder as a witness to the world of ants, I observed the markings of a wonder-less and unhealthy relationship between a parent and a child while attending my daughter's music concert. I was sitting in the audience when a family of three entered the row of seats in front of us. They sat silently for a minute or two before the mother expressed dissatisfaction to her son concerning something he had done, or was supposed to have done, before coming to the seats. The mother's frustration and anger were evident in her face and were matched by the son's response as he leaned over his father, seated between the two, to tell his mother his perspective on the situation. The exchange quickly became heated and the mother reached across her husband to grab her son by the throat, but she was restrained with her hand just inches away. This prompted her son to threaten her with a punch in the face. Exasperated by the encounter, the mother collapsed into her seat in a tension-filled posture of frustration, anger, and a tinge of helplessness. The son persisted with one more attempt to explain his position, until the father spoke for the first time, telling the boy to shut up. This ended their interaction for the time that I remained behind them.

Fortunately, most families do not feel or show such intense animosity. But this example demonstrates what can result when we lose our perspective on familial relationships. The loss of a healthy perspective on human relationships is often related to our inability to experience some form of wonder in our lives. The absence of wonder is becoming more pervasive as contemporary life seems to move more quickly and the pressures of practical concerns and responsibilities seem to rise. These pressures often overshadow the experience of wonder in the lives of parents.

Losing touch with the ability to wonder is a form of forgetfulness. This forgetfulness can turn even parental love sour. But if simple ants have the instincts to protect their young from harm, so do we. Unfortunately, the complexity of our lives and of our ability to think in different ways can lead us to overlook these primal, but healthy and essential, instincts. Sometimes we need to simplify our lives and engage in forms of thinking that may not seem practical for accomplishing everyday tasks, but are necessary for providing the perspective we need to make wise decisions. Philosophy can help us to remember how to think in different ways, to remember things that we often forget, and gain new perspectives on how we relate to our children.

Wisdom and Wonder

Although wisdom and wonder are both essential elements in the philosophical life, they are not often linked with each other directly. "Philosophy" is translated from the Greek *philo-sophia*, which literally means "the love of wisdom." As the *love* of wisdom, philosophy desires and pursues wisdom; it does not possess it. This pursuit follows many different paths, but each of these paths is a lifelong process of reflection and contemplation. Wonder, on the other hand, is traditionally thought of as the origin or source of the philosophical life. The experience of wonder generates the inquiries that lead to wisdom, but it is not usually thought of as a part of wisdom itself. The phrase "the wisdom of wonder," however, suggests that wonder is an integral part of wisdom itself, and not just the origin of an inquiry that leads to wisdom.

As parents we need to cultivate what Aristotle called practical wisdom. Practical wisdom involves the ability to deliberate well about what is good and bad for human beings in general. A person who has practical wisdom may not know how to fix a sink, work a computer, or play the stock market, but he has the capacity to think clearly about the overall good for himself and for others. Of course, there are many different opinions and points of view concerning what is good for human beings in general. In order to know what is actually good as compared to what only appears good, we must have some insight into the basic needs of human nature. That is, we must learn to differentiate between what we and our children merely want and what we really need.

Parents are more aware than most of the variety of opinions there is concerning the good for human beings. Parents are faced with the challenge of mining good decisions out of a vast landscape of possibilities for themselves and for their children. For them, insight into human nature and the difference between real human goods and illusory goods is essential for making wise decisions for themselves and their children. An appreciation of the activity of wonder can help by providing us with the space we need to have a thoughtful and healthy perspective on the good life and how to achieve it. But wonder is not highly valued in our fast-paced society, in which achieving goals and meeting appointments are revered. For parents, who are faced with meeting the challenges of professional and family life, there is little time for wonder, making it seem like a vague, far-off dream. In fact, we have become so accustomed to thinking without wonder that many question its usefulness. In order to demonstrate the importance of wonder and recover the possibility of engaging in it, we need to understand the type of thinking that resists it so forcefully. This thinking is called calculative thinking. Calculative thinking dominates the modern psyche; so much so that an imbalance has evolved in human thinking that negatively affects many of our relationships, including familial relationships.

The Calculative Mind

The calculative mind became the focal point of human consciousness in the seventeenth century through the work of the French philosopher René Descartes. Descartes thought that the human mind could achieve knowledge that is beyond all doubt. In order to do so, however, the mind would have to separate itself from the sense experiences of the body, because the senses give imperfect and unreliable perceptions of the world. In order to have scientific knowledge, according to Descartes, there can be no mystery or ambiguity in what we know. Unambiguous or scientific knowledge, therefore, must be achieved by carefully following the logical principles and procedures of reason, exclusively.

This approach to thinking and truth provided the basis for modern science by transforming our perceptions of the natural world into phenomena that can be measured mathematically. By separating human rationality from the natural order of things, Descartes effectively reduced nature to that which can be controlled and manipulated through science and technology. That is, reason became the locus of meaning and the essential part of the person. Nature became lifeless or raw material with no inherent dignity of its own.

There is no dispute over the power of calculative thinking. It has led to unimaginable progress in many areas of human life, most notably in the vast proliferation of technology. But the pervasiveness of calculative thinking and technology not only shapes the way we relate to the natural world, it has come to shape the way human beings understand themselves, and their relationships with each other. For example, some advertising campaigns use women as sexual tools to generate passionate responses in potential consumers. Free-market globalization uses economic criteria almost exclusively to determine public policy while convincing people to measure their self-worth in terms of material wealth. As a result, the dignity of human life is in as much jeopardy as the natural environment. Just as Descartes effectively extricated the life out of nature, the pervasiveness of calculative thought in the modern world is doing the same to human beings.

In trying to eliminate all mystery and ambiguity from our experience, calculative thinking makes our experience of the world self-referential. That is, we choose to see only what is measured and predictable in accordance with calculative rationality. Within the confines of calculation, we can no longer see the enchantment of the world, which is full of spontaneity, mystery, and otherness. This is dangerous. For as Sam Keen argues in *Apology for Wonder*, we cannot be authentically human without the spontaneity, mystery, and ambiguity that characterize the experience of wonder. David Abram echoes this insight in *The Spell of the Sensuous*, in which he argues that we are human only in contact, and conviviality, with what is not human. The calculative mind limits human experience to one level of human consciousness. It cannot account for, understand, or even tolerate what it cannot measure, quantify, or generate. Thus, calculative thinking cannot satisfy the human need for relationships with what is other than ourselves; relationships that are based on openness, mystery, care, and love. In fact, when calculative thinking becomes too pervasive, as it has in many areas of modern life, it gets in the way of our ability to have healthy relationships, including relationships with our children. In order to be fully human and to guide their children toward a full and healthy adult life, parents need to supplement the calculative mind by recovering a sense of wonder. In recovering the experience of wonder, parents not only recover an essential part of their own lives, they also help their children sustain the capacity for wonder as they grow and develop the capacities of reason. The type of thinking that can accomplish the healthy retrieval of wonder is contemplation.

The Contemplative Mind

There is a well-known story concerning Heraclitus, a legendary pre-Socratic philosopher from Ionia who lived around 500 B.C. It might be hard for us to imagine a philosopher being so famous that people would travel long distances just to get a glimpse of him. But apparently this was the case with Heraclitus. One particular day a group of visitors came upon the thinker unexpectedly while he was standing by the fire in his kitchen. For some reason, the visitors were startled on seeing him. Some speculate that Heraclitus was warming himself naked by the fire. Undaunted by their surprise, Heraclitus encouraged the visitors not to be shy but to come into his kitchen, because "here too the gods dwell." For Heraclitus, and for all of the great contemplative minds throughout history, the sacred and the holy are found among the familiar and mundane. The things we see and interact with on a daily basis are where the mystery and magic of life reside. For many, the magic and mystery of the modern world is hidden behind the obsession with certainty and material gratification. Our capacity to perceive the ambiguous depths and latencies of the familiar is diminished under the spell of technological innovation, titillating entertainment, and copious consumption.

The contemplative mind does not shy away from what cannot be quantified. The contemplative mind welcomes and dwells in mystery. A virtue of the contemplative mind is its ability to welcome and appreciate the ambiguity that is present in what it perceives. Contemplation is open, nonjudgmental, and receptive. When we direct a contemplative gaze toward something, we do not impose our will on it, but rather we allow the other to emerge and fully express itself. The contemplative mind preserves an awareness of the ambiguous background from which individual figures emerge, in contrast to the calculative mind, which seeks a clear representation or concept of what it perceives. As the calculative mind intensifies its focus on an individual object, it tends to ignore the contextual background from which the individual object emerges. As a result, it misses the depth, meaning, and fluid presence that dwell in the background. The familiar things of everyday life become lifeless and uneventful when we no longer perceive the depths from which they emerge. The contemplative mind has the capacity to perceive these depths and, as a result, in the contemplation of ordinary things we encounter the sacred and holy. This is what enabled Heraclitus to encounter gods even in his kitchen.

But I doubt that Heraclitus had children. The kitchen in my house is often a battleground where strong wills clash; it does not usually feel like an abode for the sacred and the holy. Most often these contests arise between my wife and one of our two daughters. Dinnertime, for instance, is often preceded by negotiation. As the minutes leading up to dinner pass and the food cools, the intensity of my wife's and daughters' willfulness grows and negotiations become full-fledged standoffs. On bad days these standoffs can result in a mother's raised voice and a child's tears. But parents have the power to derive positive outcomes from these standoffs by maintaining a contemplative mind and a broad perspective, rather than locking heads with their children. In our house the parent who is lucky enough not to be locked in a battle of wills can often find a calm, peaceful way out. This is easier for the parent who is not intensely engaged because he or she is not faced with the invitation to respond to each assertion the child makes. Instead, this parent can see and hear more than the specific words of the dialogue. He or she can perceive the background or unconscious factors that contribute to the child's resistance by maintaining a contemplative perspective. For instance, the child may not be hungry. She may be tired and may not feel comfortable sitting. She may be feeling lonely or hurt by something she saw at school. She may need more intimate attention. These are things the child may not be able to express in words, and this may lead to even further frustration and anger. As a result, a parent may not be able to perceive the source of the child's resistance while trying to serve dinner.

The nonengaged parent has an opportunity to be more contemplative. This makes it possible not only to better understand the child's perspective, but also to better understand the frustration of his or her partner. This frustration may be caused by more than just the child's resistance to sit at the dinner table. A mother may be tired. She may have been interrupted too many times during the day and, as a result, may have failed to get all of her work done. She may have unpaid bills hanging over her head. She may be feeling unfulfilled as a result of spending too much time with children and not enough with adults. The unconscious factors of behavior are complex and deep and it helps when there is someone to help us become aware of them, especially when dealing with children.

To perceive these unconscious factors, the contemplative parent needs composure, patience, and wonder, not a will to control or judge. By relinquishing the need to control, parents can hear the background voices that drive their child's behavior as well as their own. As we open up to the background influences on behavior, we begin to see the burdens a child carries as she makes her way through the day. We feel compassion for the child as we help her to decipher her moods and emotions. Guided by compassion, rather than a will to control, we hold and hug the child even as she vents her frustration at us. We help her to become comfortable with complex feelings and forces that she barely understands. In abandoning the impulse to control the situation, we are better able to decipher what the child is expressing in her moods, gestures, and words. Such understanding is not possible if we focus on and respond to only her words. It requires a compassionate, emotionally attuned receptiveness to the child. Real understanding will occur if we love our children and allow them to love themselves, even when they don't want either form of love. As we will examine in later chapters, love is the human means of self-transcendence into the holy and the sacred. So even on kitchen battlegrounds, we, like Heraclitus, can create a space in which the divine can dwell.

Hence the experience of the mysterious, the sacred, and the holy is not limited to the few contemplative minds we learn about by studying our intellectual history. Well-known thinkers and spiritual seekers have given us models by which we can understand and develop the contemplative life; they also make it clear that this life is available to all human beings. In fact, I am sure that many parents have had experiences of the sacred and the holy in watching their children grow, create, and flourish in the world. But our world is very different from the world of ancient Greece, in which philosophers and the activity of contemplation were revered. Parents who work, cook, and chauffeur their children from event to event do not have the time to develop their capacity for contemplation and, as a result, their experience of wonder is often fragmented. Yet, we are never far removed from genuine experiences of wonder, because these experiences are called forth by a confrontation with the mysterious depth of meaning at the heart of what is familiar.[1] And what could be more familiar to a parent than her child? When we take the time to step back from the world of calculation, organization, and moneymaking, we can see in our children what children so often see in the world—an embodiment of the mysterious and the sacred.

Celebrating Snow

To see children in this light and to see what children see is not easy. In attempting to meet everyday responsibilities and to make wise decisions on behalf of their children, parents are often frustrated by the lack of foresight that is endemic in childhood and adolescence. Recently my wife and I experienced this frustration as we were trying to get our two daughters to a birthday party. They were dressed in shoes and stockings, which made it a bad idea to walk through the twelve inches of snow that had fallen a couple of days earlier. The prospect of them sitting in a car with wet and cold feet was not pleasant. At best, they would be uncomfortable. They might also get sick. The additional concern of arriving at the party on time determined that we did not want them to get wet and then have to change their clothes. Keeping the girls out of the snow seemed like the practical and wise thing to do. But the bright, clean, soft snow was beckoning, and our four-year-old couldn't resist.

As I thought about the ineffectiveness of my negotiation to keep her from the snow, I began to realize that the reasons I gave her might have made sense from an adult's perspective, but not from a child's. While we were trying to guide her with practical wisdom, my daughter was guided by wonder. The snow was alluring to her. In responding to the allure of the snow, she was not concerned about the value of dry shoes and socks or the need to be on time for a birthday party. For her, these are incidental concerns, which do not excite or attract her in the way that fresh snow does. The reasons I gave to convince her to stay out of the snow made no sense in her wonder-filled world. I was guided by the practical concerns that infuse conventional adult wisdom; dry socks are better than wet socks. She was guided by the more powerful allure of the snow's natural beauty.

Many parents who have experienced this type of frustration regard children's proclivity for wonder as a passing phase that they will grow out of when they gain a more mature understanding of the world. But the experience of wonder should not be dismissed as the mere fancy of an immature mind. Wonder is the wellspring of allurement or attraction. As Brian Swimme points out, allurement is *the* primal force that holds together the entire universe. From the smallest electromagnetic particles to the largest galaxies, the force of allurement or attraction sustains all entities and communities in the universe. This primal force is not something we can explain. It is a mysterious fact of the universe.[2] Within the macrocosmic universe, human beings are motivated and drawn by their own set of attractions. Just as electromagnetic particles are attracted to each other, human beings are attracted to many different things, such as a type of music, a type of person, or snow. Thus, even as adults, when we examine just why we are attracted to a particular thing, or why we are attracted to anything at all, we come face to face with one of the great mysteries of the universe.

Hence, a child's sense of wonder is not, and should not be regarded as, a mere passing phase. Children who have the opportunity to respond to wonder are experiencing and manifesting the primal, mysterious reality of the universe. The same force of attraction that binds the universe and its multitude of beings and communities together guides the child toward her source of wonder. By responding to this wonder, the child is discovering and creatively expressing her personality, who she is and who she can become. As parents we need to be aware of the effect of our interventions, because they might end up stifling a child's passionate and creative response to wonder.

Also, when we fail to respond to or engage in wonder, or deny a child the opportunity to respond to wonder, we miss an opportunity to discover our creative potential and, ultimately, our personal and communal destiny. It is not surprising, then, that thinking about allurement as a fundamental law of the universe gives me pause when I begin to guide my daughter away from snow banks. The snow is enchanting for her, and this is why she needs to walk through it. She is responding to wonder, and, in doing so, she allows her deepest self, the mysterious seeds of attraction that define who she is and who she will become, to be called forth into the light of day. By preventing or discouraging children from engaging their source of wonder, we can cause them to become confused and doubtful about the importance of what excites them. To interrupt their sense of wonder is to dampen the sparks of passion that they need to nurture if they are to discover who they want and need to be. A parent's world of practical concerns becomes utterly impractical and unwise if it does not provide the space for children to discover their creativity and pursue their passions.

As I thought about my daughter frolicking in the snow, I began to realize that for her it is not necessary to be at a birthday party to celebrate. For her, celebration is a natural and spontaneous way to respond to the world as much as to scheduled events. Things that seem familiar or even a nuisance to adults, such as a January snowfall, are enchanting, celebratory events for children. Whereas we want to put the snowfall behind us as soon as possible, four-year-old children see it as something that calls for their participation. They do not calculate the consequences of getting wet. Instead they choose to explore the mysteriousness of their world, which is now covered with cold, soft, white stuff. In responding to the allure of the snow, children enjoy one of the gifts of childhood, which is the capacity for sustained delight.

As adults, we know that dry shoes and socks are valid concerns that a young child may not understand. As parents we have a responsibility to help children to understand these concerns, and when they cannot we must make decisions for them. But we often forget to ask what we fail to see in the child's perspective when we neglect, ignore, or suppress the allure of wonder that is so natural to children. In many cases, parents avoid the experience of wonder and shut down a child's instinct for wonder because it seemingly doesn't make good sense or it is inconvenient. To allow oneself or one's child to become engaged by the allure of wonder can disrupt a well-planned day or add extra work, such as changing clothes or giving an extra bath. But if a practically wise parent is one who has the capacity to act for the overall good of herself and her children, it makes sense to better understand the capacities of thinking and perceiving that lead to and sustain wonder. The ability to sustain conscious presence is essential for engaging in experiences of genuine wonder.

Conscious Presence

I recently had a conversation with a highly successful financial executive on Wall Street who was about to become a father for the first time. Our conversation was wide ranging, as we were trying to understand the ways in which philosophy could enhance the workplace. After discussing some of the central virtues that I thought were relevant to this task, he raised an important question about time. He was concerned that there just didn't seem to be enough time in each day to do the things that he needed to do, and with his first child coming this bothered him. In response to his question, I pointed out the irony that seems to have emerged with the proliferation of technology. Technology originated as a means of alleviating our workload. With technological devices, it was assumed, we could reduce the time it takes to perform the necessary tasks of labor and free ourselves up to explore more fulfilling tasks. As the most recent economic statistics show, however, the opposite seems to have occurred. We work more hours for less real wages than we did twenty years ago. People feel as though they have greater stress and less time than ever before. In effect, we seem to be losing time, which means we are losing our lives. Even as modern medicine extends biological life, our actual experience of the world, of life, seems to be growing shorter. The questions is, Where does time go?

To answer this question, we need only think back to the last time we drove our car somewhere. We may remember getting into the car and we may remember arriving at our destination. But unless something unusual happened along the way, we probably do not remember much about the actual journey. While driving, we tend to lose ourselves in daydreams or musings about the past and future. The actual present—where we are at any point along the journey—is absent from consciousness. The absence of consciousness is also prevalent among workers who find little meaning in their job. These workers constantly look forward to the end of the day, literally wishing for time, their lifetime, to go faster. They dream about the weekend and try to block the workday from consciousness.

Of course, making a living is a necessity, and many have little choice in where they work. In fact, just making a living is becoming increasingly difficult for middle- and lower-middle-class workers. As a result, human beings must devote much of their attention to procuring the means to buy food and provide themselves with shelter. For many people, this process has come to so dominate their attention that they find themselves with little time for anything else.

But this is unhealthy, because people have needs to be met and capacities to be developed that go beyond the basic necessities of food and shelter. These needs and capacities call out to be nurtured and developed through meaningful activities in which consciousness is present, not absent. Yet, mysteriously, when presented with an opportunity to pursue such activities, we often choose absentmindedness. We tend to ignore or suppress the need (ours and our children's) for meaningful and creative self-expression. We often find ourselves saying that we don't have the time to wonder, to play with our children, to exercise, to meditate. We lose our physical, mental, and spiritual health while making ourselves more and more busy. We worry about the future and the past and dream of how life could be different than it is. People in all walks of life find themselves perpetually longing for a better day, failing to find fulfillment in the present. And this is where we lose our time, because human time is conscious time.[3]

The loss of time that is so common in our culture is not new. It has been depicted throughout the great literary and spiritual traditions as the most painful of human experiences. Jacob Needleman points out that the Hebrew term *Sheol* refers to "dark, weak existence, continually fading, ever-paler life."[4] *Sheol* is the realm of diminishing being. In the context of contemporary life, *Sheol* can be understood as the condition of ever-diminishing human presence or conscious presence. As we create ever more desires and as technology replaces human beings in the means of production, we become further and further removed from those activities in which human beings find real meaning. We lose essential outlets for creative self-expression behind the distracting lights of electronic devices and the insidious allure of unnecessary goods. Our capacity for creative self-expression, which was traditionally realized in various means of production and play, has been separated from the activities of daily life and hence severely compromised. As a result, the impulses and instincts for creative and meaningful self-expression are pushed into the depths of consciousness. From there they often force their way into the light of day in ways that are detrimental to the personality.

The God of the Old Testament can be understood as a forceful response to these forms of human absence and lifelessness. When Moses asked God what he should tell the people when they asked him who sent him with the commandments, God responded, "Say unto the children of Israel, I AM hath sent me unto you." Whereas *Sheol* is the condition of ever-increasing lifelessness and absence, God is "I AM," or conscious presence in the midst of life. In a very real and effective way, *Sheol* describes the absent state of the human psyche, which can be understood as a modern-day experience of diminishing being, the loss of life, or even hell. In contrast, conscious presence is the opening to the sacred in the world. Unfortunately, the conditions of our culture favor the diminishing of Being, as it becomes less and less necessary for human beings to be consciously present to accomplish the tasks that we are obliged to perform.

To achieve conscious presence we must heighten our awareness of the many factors that shape our lives. We need to listen for the meaning in the background voices, our own and those of others, to better understand what motivates and attracts us. We need to resist the temptation of the idle mind to be carried away by the flashy, tantalizing messages of consumerist culture. And we also need to be aware of the benefits and limits of fantasizing or dreaming about the past or future. While fantasies and dreams can be an important part of adult life, they work against us if they serve as a mere escape from or avoidance of the simple and difficult realities we face in the everyday world. They are most effective when they help us to gain alternative perspectives on the world, both the interior world of the unconscious and the external reality of the world with which we interact. As an escape mechanism dreams and fantasies pull us away from conscious presence. As alternative perspectives on our lives and the world in which we live, they can enhance conscious presence.

By cultivating conscious presence we become more attuned to what is occurring in and around ourselves at any given moment and allow ourselves to be moved and affected by others. The openness that characterizes conscious presence serves as an antidote to the familiar impulse to control. It offers a challenge to one's own presuppositions and expectations and overturns them when warranted. This is what enables human beings to transcend the self-referential confines of the calculative mind and to experience the sacred depths of others and the world. Unlike children, whose wonder is free to explore the fantasies of play and imagination, adults usually require a concerted effort to step out of the persuasive current of practical affairs to engage in play and imagination. Without a disciplined effort to step back from everyday adult concerns, it is difficult to see the intricate details of the world that give rise to genuine experiences of wonder. Conscious presence is a mature, disciplined way to see the world through the lens of adult wonder.

To be effective, conscious presence must also involve emotional awareness. In order to be consciously present to another or to a situation, we need to open our own emotional vaults and allow ourselves to be affected by what we see and hear. For example (as we will explore in chapter 4), listening requires much more than working ears. It requires a willingness to open oneself to the other and to be affected by what the other communicates through words, gestures, moods, and feelings. Such openness provides the space for another person to reveal herself in all of her mystery and depth. And it is the mystery and depth of others and of the world in general that invite the experience of wonder. To be open in this way requires conscious presence in place of a willful ego. Through conscious presence we recover human time. We restore our lives.

There is no area of life in which conscious presence is more crucial than in parenting. While my discussion of conscious presence impressed the Wall Street executive, he was still faced with the problem of the amount of hours he had to put in to succeed at his career. If he was to maintain the level of success he had achieved, he would not be at home very often, and, no matter how consciously aware he was, it would not benefit his child. This is an issue that most working parents wrestle with throughout their lives. And while there are no easy solutions, the primary question parents need to think about is what it means to their children and to themselves to be consciously present. To jump-start this process, let us reflect on three versions of parental presence that are familiar in today's world.

Three Portraits of Parental Presence

John is an all-city baseball player for a leading prep school in New York City. As a sophomore he was the starting catcher on the varsity team. The word about John's talent spread during his freshman year, when Mr. Beck, his religious studies teacher, went to see him play. Over the course of more than thirty years of teaching, during which he has taught more than four thousand students, Mr. Beck has seen many talented students cross his path. In his opinion, John was one of the best. Mr. Beck attended as many games as he could during John's career at the prep. He reveled in watching other teams intentionally walk John in crucial situations or hesitate on the base paths because of the strength and accuracy of John's throwing arm. John was a pleasure to watch and was a major factor in transforming an otherwise mediocre team into a championship team.

Mr. Beck became familiar with the core group of parents who were regulars at the games. As Mr. Beck saw it, these parents were not so much fulfilling their parental duty as they were reaping their parental rewards. They were seeing firsthand that their hard-earned money was preparing their children for college, but the games also gave them an opportunity to share in the development of their children. Unfortunately, John's parents were not a part of the group of parents that regularly attended games. In fact, they never saw John play. Their hard-earned money may have been going to the right school to prepare John for college, but they were not present to watch that preparation unfold. While John's talent inspired awe in his opponents and teachers, his parents could only hear about it from others. His parents were not only consciously absent; they were physically absent. They not only relied on the school environment to protect, preserve, and stimulate John's development; they were missing one of the most moving and rewarding experiences of being a parent—watching their son flourish as he pursued his passion. They were missing the content of their son's life, and those years would pass in what seemed like an instant.

As long as a parent is physically absent, conscious presence is impossible. With the work schedule of many parents, physical presence is a real challenge. However, physical presence does not ensure conscious presence. A couple of years ago my psychologist friend was visiting, and we were having a discussion in the living room. My daughter was two at the time, and she was in the room with us. We interrupted our conversation numerous times to address her with a few words, a hug, or a smile. This worked well for a while. We could talk about Habermas or Tillich and she seemed happy to be in the room with us. After a half hour or so I asked my friend if he wanted a glass of water or a beer. He said he would have something and simultaneously we stood up and walked to the kitchen. As we were about to turn the corner into the kitchen, my daughter cried as hard as I had ever heard her cry. I turned quickly to see if she had fallen or if something had fallen on her, but she was sitting in the middle of the room, and there was nothing around that could have hurt her. The psychologist and the philosopher were heartily embarrassed to realize that she was devastated by our cold indifference, our rudeness, as we walked out on her without saying where or why we were going.

We were shamed by the realization that we had been paying attention to her only to facilitate our own desire to converse. Once our attention shifted from our conversation, we also forgot about her. We were not consciously present for her, though we deceived her into thinking otherwise by occasionally giving her token attention while we talked about something else.

Now, adults need to talk, and appeasing toddlers to do so is not a bad thing. But appeasing them without being aware of what they might be thinking, without being conscious of what we are leading them to think or feel, is irresponsible and potentially hurtful. Our tactic in this case was a product of the calculative mind, insofar as we were procuring a space for conversation. But as the end result demonstrates, the calculative mind can cause us to overlook the child's perspective and lead to hurtful behavior. To be consciously present is to have an awareness of the child's perspective and to use that awareness to inform how we respond to the child.

My wife was talking to her friend Joan recently about the swimming lessons her son was taking. Joan was extremely pleased with the lessons but cautioned my wife that they were intensive and would require a lot of her time. The lessons were twice a week, about fifteen miles away. Joan confessed that because of the travel, there were times when she thought about pulling her son out, but she persevered. Joan watched each session intently, noticing minor progress for five or six weeks. One night, she stepped away from the pool for a moment to use the rest room, and on returning she watched her son completing his first lap of the pool by himself. Her emotions overwhelmed her, and she welled up with tears. Her child was gliding across a body of water for the first time and she was his witness. She watched him execute a skill that would be a part of him for the rest of his life, and she felt the magnitude of his accomplishment for and with him. Her tears were not the tears of an overemotional mother. Rather, they were the visible expression of the deep emotional connection she has with her son. In identifying with her son's accomplishment, she transcended the confines of her own subjectivity, of her own concerns.

Joan's experience displays many of the qualities associated with a genuine experience of wonder. For instance, the distinction between subject and object was broken down, so that her being was identified with the event. Her son was a presence rather than an object. This presence generated a cognitive and an emotional response. The event came without explanation, like a revelation. It appeared as if by chance, unexpectedly, bringing new meaning that could not immediately be integrated into past patterns of understanding and explanation. Finally, her wonder was called forth by a confrontation with the mysterious depths of meaning at the heart of the familiar. For Joan, these depths were found in her child swimming for the first time, which she witnessed with reverence and love. These qualities of perception are typical in an experience of wonder, and they allow us to feel that the world is sacred and holy. Joan encountered the sacred and the holy through the accomplishment of her son. Her presence, both physical and conscious, led to a genuine experience of wonder.

Wonder-full Wisdom

When we situate human consciousness in the context of billions of years of cosmic evolution, we realize that we are a very young species. We are only beginning to find our way and purpose in the cosmological event. Despite our relative inexperience, we are confident that our primary purpose has something to do with our ability to think reflectively. That is, we are capable of self-consciousness. We can stand back from our existence and observe what we are and what we do. As far as we can tell, there is no other species or mode of consciousness that has this ability. So in the context of the cosmos as a whole, we are the eyes and ears through which the universe knows itself. We are the species that makes the universe aware of its beauty, power, destructiveness, and potential. Before self-reflexive awareness emerged on Earth, there were majestic occurrences taking place, such as ice ages coming and going, mountains forming, and new plants and species being born. But no one or no thing was consciously aware of the awesome magnitude and mystery of these events until human beings became self-reflexive beings.

This is an awesome responsibility that human beings have inherited. And it directly parallels the awesome responsibility that we have as parents of our children. Children have no idea of the beauty and potential they embody. The primary function of a parent, therefore, is to see and hear their beauty and grace, to make them aware of their majesty and their potential, and to give them the confidence to trust in their own abilities and to pursue their passionate interests. Who cannot see the tragedy of a child who has no one to feel and cherish her beauty, to fall in love with her, and to celebrate her splendor?[5]

John may have been an all-city baseball player. But the absence of his parents had to leave an emptiness that could not be filled, even by the special appreciation of a devoted teacher. On the other hand, by perceiving the majesty and mystery of her son's accomplishment, Joan was instilling a deep sense of self-trust in her son. She was making her son aware of his own importance and the importance of his accomplishments. She was teaching him to trust his own sense of allurement and to have the confidence to pursue his interests. These are things children cannot know about themselves unless those who do know make them aware of them. This awareness is the *wisdom of wonder* that parents need to experience and share with their children if they are to guide their children beyond the trials and pitfalls of emotional, psychological, and physical development.

So the experience of wonder is an essential element in the acquisition and implementation of practical wisdom, because it enables parents to perceive the mystery and depth of their children and of the world in general. Guided by a spirit of reverence and love, which arise out of the experience of wonder, parents can gain unique insights into the mysterious and sacred nature of their children and of the world. With this awareness, parents are better able to make practically wise decisions for their children and for themselves.

In discussing the role of wonder in achieving practical wisdom, we have given a preliminary account of human nature and the primary function of parents. Aristotle believed that it is essential to understand human nature and its function if we are to achieve our highest goal, which is happiness. Let us now turn to this most central of human concerns as a way to better understand what we really want for our children.

Notes

1. Sam Keen, *Apology for Wonder* (New York: Harper and Collins, 1980), 14.
2. Brian Swimme, *The Universe Is a Green Dragon* (Santa Fe, N.Mex.: Bear, 1984), 45.
3. Swimme, *The Universe Is a Green Dragon*, 33.
4. Jacob Needleman, *Money and the Meaning of Life* (New York: Doubleday, 1984).
5. Swimme, *The Universe Is a Green Dragon*, 15.

CHAPTER TWO

The Habits of Happiness

One of my favorite children's movies of recent years is *Toy Story 2*. Like most good movies, *Toy Story 2* can be enjoyed on many levels. Children identify and laugh with the colorful animated characters, while adults can interpret various scenes as commentaries on life's central concerns. In the climactic scene of the movie we find the main character, Woody, faced with an existential choice about how he will spend his future. Woody is a toy cowboy, and he is the favorite toy of a boy named Andy. Woody's troubles begin when he bravely tries to rescue another toy, Weezy the penguin, from being sold in a yard sale. While outside making the rescue, Woody is spotted by Al, a toy collector, who recognizes Woody as a classic toy. Al needs Woody to complete a set of toys called *Woody's Roundup*. If he acquires Woody, he will sell the set to a museum for a large amount of money. Andy's mother refuses to sell Woody, because she knows how important he is to her son. Not to be denied, Al the toy collector steals Woody and speeds away in the hopes of making a quick and profitable sale.

Woody doesn't know how famous he is until he is united with the other members of *Woody's Roundup*. Al has locked up these toys in storage. They have been waiting for the day when Woody would be found so that as a group they could get out of storage. Woody is their ticket to freedom. There is, however, one fundamental problem. Woody's idea of freedom is very different from the others' idea of freedom. For the toys that have been kept in storage, being put on display in a museum seems like a great opportunity. Woody, on the other hand, wants to be reunited with Andy, who loves him dearly,

31

and with his other toy friends at Andy's house. If he returns to Andy, however, the other members of *Woody's Roundup* will never get out of storage, since they are valuable only as a set. Jessie the cowgirl and the Prospector try to persuade Woody to stay by reminding him that children lose interest in toys as they grow older. As much as Andy loves Woody now, that love will not last, and Woody will be left behind. Jessie the cowgirl knows this because it happened to her.

This line of reasoning softens Woody's stance about returning to Andy. The other toys then make him feel guilty by reminding him that if he leaves they will remain in boxes. After a while, Woody becomes convinced that staying with the group is the right thing to do. After all, he thinks, if he stays he won't have to go through the pain of being separated from someone he loves.

While Jessie and the Prospector work at changing Woody's mind, his toy friends from Andy's house are zeroing in on his location for the rescue. When they finally find Woody, after avoiding great peril to get there, they are confused and disappointed to learn that Woody is thinking of staying. Buzz Lightyear, the most determined of the rescue team, challenges the reasons for which Woody would stay. Intuitively, Buzz knows that Woody has to clarify for himself what he understands to be his proper purpose or function in life. Without a clear understanding of this purpose or function, it would be difficult to make a good decision about his future. To assist Woody, Buzz reminds him of his own words, expressed to Buzz some time earlier. Woody told Buzz that the purpose of being a toy is to be loved by a child. If a toy can achieve that goal, even for a short while, it is infinitely better than to never have been loved. To go to a museum as an object to be observed by many, but to never again be loved by a child, would be to skirt his proper purpose in life. This would inevitably result in an unfulfilled, unhappy existence. Having been reminded of his own wisdom by Buzz, Woody not only agrees to escape himself, but convinces Jessie the cowgirl and Bullseye the toy horse to go with him to Andy's house.

The Prospector has a different view of things. The Prospector is a bearded toy who was never removed from his box. He has never experienced the love of a child, so the prospect of getting to a museum is good enough for him. At least he will be let out of his box, and spectators passing through will admire him. This will surely be a happier existence than the one he has known. The different life experiences of Woody and the Prospector give them very different ideas of their proper purpose and of what constitutes a good life. As a result they choose very different behavioral paths.

This story raises a number of important issues concerning the good life and the cultivation of habits that are conducive to such a life. As we work our way toward an understanding of happiness and how parents can foster the happiness of their children, we will refer to this story and place some of the ideas it presents in dialogue with important thinkers, most prominently, the ancient Greek philosopher Aristotle.

Happiness as the Highest Good

Aristotle begins the *Nicomachean Ethics* by pointing out that we human beings pursue many goods in our everyday activities. The various goods we seek are teleological. That is, lesser goods lead or contribute to higher goods. Ideally, all of the lesser goods that we pursue lead to happiness, the highest human good.

Most people agree that happiness is their highest aim, but many have different opinions concerning the true nature of happiness. Because of this diversity of opinions concerning happiness, it is essential to identify false notions of happiness that can seduce us into thinking they are the real thing. The most common mistake that people make is to confuse the life of pleasure with a genuinely happy life. While pleasure is an essential part of a good and happy life, it is not the same thing as happiness. Anyone who has spent too much time pursuing pleasures is familiar with the pain that follows their achievement. In fact, there are many pleasurable things that can lead to a very unhappy life, which makes it clear that pleasure and happiness are not the same thing.

But there are other imposters of happiness that are very tempting, such as a life of honor, wealth, health, or even virtue. Like pleasure, these things can contribute to and are even essential for living the good life, but none taken by itself can constitute the highest human happiness. Each of these goods is a means to the higher goal of happiness, whereas happiness is never a means to anything higher. Happiness stands alone as that to which everything else aims. Thus happiness is an end in itself, never a means to some other end.

Another unique quality of the happy life or the happy person is its consistency and perseverance. Happiness persists over time and is only minimally affected by external circumstances. The happy individual remains happy throughout life because he can respond to any situation in the appropriate way. Each response to each situation comes from a highly developed character and disposition that takes pleasure from doing what is virtuous or noble. So even in the most difficult or unpleasant circumstances, the actions of the happy man will add to his happiness rather than detract from it.

Finally, happiness is not something that we own or something that we acquire as a permanent quality. Happiness is a direct result of the activities we engage in and the way in which we act. Only by acting, not by observing or by avoiding action, can we experience the happy life. The idle person cannot be happy. It is by acting that we develop the ability to act appropriately in any situation. Over time, through virtuous repetition, we develop habits of virtuous behavior. Hence, virtue, excellence, and appropriateness become our spontaneous mode of response to the world.

As parents, we are entrusted to guide children toward a happy and good life. To be effective, we must be aware of the false notions of happiness that buzz through the minds of children each day. Children are pulled in different directions by new promises of pleasures and honor in their modern forms of consumerism and public recognition or spurious peer acceptance. We must not only warn them away from these imposters, we must also provide positive alternatives that will attract and hold their interest. Only with positive alternatives to the base values on which popular culture thrives can children sustain the right kinds of activities and develop confident, virtuous habits of behavior. To this end, parents must convince children that their self-worth cannot be found in short-term pleasures, material goods, or trendy friends. While it may be inevitable that some children will, at times, gauge their self-worth through the eyes of public acceptance and recognition, it is devastating for children when parents measure their children's happiness through the deceptive lens of these imposters.

Honoring First Communion Day

A few years ago I attended my niece's first communion. She and her classmates were six or seven years old. With my own relationship to the religion of my childhood strained and confused, I looked at the day as an opportunity to recover the enchantment of ceremony that shaped my childhood. I gazed on the scene with pleasure as the young boys and girls recited their prayers with enthusiasm and responded attentively to the promptings of their teacher to kneel and stand when appropriate. The priest did his best to make the mystery of a Trinitarian God and a resurrection meaningful to children. But as hard as I tried to quell the cynic in me, something was preventing me from giving myself over to the scene completely. Then I went outside, where any hope for a Kierkegaardian leap from cynicism to faith was lost. As we filed from the church, I noticed traffic in the parking lot was stalled behind three stretch limousines. I hadn't noticed any dignitaries inside the church, but I waited to see if I had missed something. To my amazement, I watched three of the children who had just received their first communion each climb into a limousine. The limousine bug had descended from prom night to first communion day.

We need to honor important events in the lives of children. In doing so, we help them to distinguish what is significant from what is less significant, while making them aware of the importance of their own lives. However, the way in which we honor our children is crucial to their sense of self and to their expectations about the future. If a six-year-old child's first communion warrants a stretch limousine, what will his graduation require to make him or the event seem worthwhile? Recalling Aristotle's insights into false accounts of happiness, we might interpret the parents' gesture in this case as an attempt to facilitate the happiness of their children by providing both honor and pleasure through the extravagant act of hiring limousines. The danger, of course, is that the children can easily confuse the significance of the vehicle used to honor them with the meaning of the event for which they are being honored. If this becomes a pattern, a child can quickly become like the king described by the French mathematician and philosopher Blaise Pascal. All of the king's subjects brought him gifts unceasingly. The more gifts he accepted, the more gifts he needed to be satisfied. But he soon realized that he had become what Buddhists refer to as the hungry ghost. He had an insatiable appetite for things but no substance to himself. His attachment to things caused him to forget who he was as a person. He could only see himself through his gifts. In our age of hyperconsumerism, parents are incessantly challenged to avoid the danger of honoring our children through external goods and rewards, because in doing so we can easily and quickly diminish a child's sense of self. A child with a diminished sense of self is not only unhappy as a child, but also faces an uphill battle in the pursuit of happiness as an adult.

So happiness is not health, wealth, honor, virtue, or pleasure. It is a function of our activities. But which activities are we talking about? Aristotle thought that the proper activity of human beings who want to achieve happiness has to be tied to reason, since reason is what is most distinctive about human beings. It is through the activity of reason (in accordance with virtue) that we experience genuine happiness. More specifically, it is when reason is engaged in the act of contemplation that we fulfill our highest potential. In Aristotle's view, contemplation is the activity of God, and, to the extent that we contemplate, we imitate or participate in the divine.

Aristotle is in great company when he suggests that human beings reach their highest levels of fulfillment by relating to the divine, or that which is greater than them. Many philosophers agree that human beings are fundamentally relational beings. That is, our nature is shaped by and has a need to engage in interpersonal, social, and spiritual relationships. But not everyone agrees that the highest and most fulfilling mode of relating is experienced exclusively through the activity of reason or contemplation. In fact, I think Sheriff Woody has something to add to Aristotle here. For Woody, the purpose of being a toy is to be in loving relationships. By fulfilling this function, Woody and the other toys are able to find their highest fulfillment. But Woody is not alone. Aristotle's teacher, Plato, as well as the entire tradition of Christianity, sees the highest level of human fulfillment as achieved through relationships based on love. In his famous dialogue called the *Symposium*, Plato describes love as a spirit that allows human beings to communicate with the gods. In the New Testament Gospel of John and in the Epistles of Paul, we are told that we can encounter the divine through loving relationships. In chapter 1 we saw that allurement is a fundamental law of the universe. Love is a force for self-transcendence. It permeates the entire cosmos, and by nurturing this force in our children and ourselves, we become attuned to the highest and deepest levels of existence and human fulfillment. So genuine happiness can be experienced not only through contemplation, as Aristotle thought, but also through love.

To the extent that contemplation opens human awareness to the mystery and wonder of life, it is essential to a healthy human existence. But a close observation of children reveals that, despite the absence of self-reflexive reason, their world, perhaps more than the typical adult's world, is full of mystery and wonder. Therefore, by identifying the function of a healthy childhood, which is not based on the life of reason, we can supplement Aristotle's account of the fully realized, supremely happy life and provide a more comprehensive account of human happiness. In doing so, we will call into question Aristotle's assumption that the way to identify the function of a species or members of a species is to isolate and separate that species by identifying in it a distinctive human characteristic. It is clear that the consciousness of young children is prerational, but it is not clear that children have no essential connection to the divine or that they do not experience genuine happiness. Hence we will follow Aristotle's methodology and attempt to gain some insight into the function of childhood. But we will modify Aristotle's presupposition that this function hinges on a fully developed faculty of reason.

The Function of a Child

In chapter 1 we briefly discussed the primary function of a parent, which is to help children to become aware of their beauty and their potential. We are the eyes through which children see who they are and who they can become. The way in which we receive and respond to them, in their accomplishments and their failures, plays a significant and enduring role in the formation of their character. The way we receive and respond to children is never neutral.

Our expectations of children contribute to and shape what they express, how they express it, and how they see themselves. These expectations are based on our idea of what children ought to be doing. Therefore, if we are to guide children toward the highest levels of human fulfillment, we should have an idea of their primary function. Without such an idea, we are likely to have misplaced expectations, which are likely to lead to inappropriate parental responses and hinder the development of a child.

Play

While it is somewhat artificial to reduce the complex developmental processes of children to one or two functions, the activity of play and the need for resistance are essential to the healthy development of a child. In fact, play is not only a universal trait of young human beings; it is common to the young of all primates. Through play, children articulate the seeds of creativity that are waiting to be fertilized. In the realm of play children experience the freedom to express those parts of their personalities that often remain dormant in nonplayful situations. When I listen in on my daughters playing, I am often astonished to learn the complexity and depth of their feelings, their concerns, and their understanding of social situations.

My youngest daughter, Anna, is two and a half years old. She is much quieter than her older sister, which sometimes makes it more difficult to know what she is thinking or feeling. She surprised us all recently when she was given the chance to do some painting at her tots program. At the time my wife was entering the third trimester of her pregnancy. Anna painted her mother's round belly in blue, the color of her shirt that day, with another round entity inside of the belly painted in green. The green mass represented the "baby in mommy's belly." I cannot remember a time when Anna initiated any conversation about the baby before or after the painting. Yet, the presence of the baby was prominent in some part of her consciousness. If she had not been given the opportunity to creatively express what was on her mind, neither she nor those around her would ever have known just how important the new presence was to her.

Of course play is not always so pleasant. Since the birth of our third child, Anna and her older sister, Caitriona, have become much more contentious in their play. Caitriona is more possessive with her toys and seems to be less kind to Anna. I suspect that Caitriona feels anxiety about her role in the family having been displaced for a second time, first with the birth of her sister and now her brother. She knows that it would be unacceptable to treat the baby unkindly, so she transfers the anxiety his presence causes onto her sister. She knows that she can usually get her way with Anna while not being seen as too unkind, because Anna can resist just enough to keep adults at bay. Anna is also using play as a means for coping with her displacement. As a two-and-a-half-year-old, she is just emerging out of her baby stage. Seeing the attention her baby brother gets, she periodically regresses into playing the infant she was a short time ago, hoping that she might recover some of the attention and comfort she enjoyed then.

At a fundamental level life itself is play. Or, more accurately, perhaps, play is responsible for life. The profusion of Being and beauty of which we are a part is the outcome of play, risk, and adventure. From minute particles to complex organisms, all are seeking adventure. Through their adventures they join with other compatible organisms to create new life, new beings. This process of play has been going on for billions of years. For human beings, the elements of surprise, excitement, and adventure are often more intense, because we are aware of the limits of life. We are aware of our own mortality. We know that we must express ourselves within a limited time span, and we do so with urgency. Our awareness of the incessant approach of our own death intensifies play activities as those through which we find our deepest self-expression. Hence, play is not only the primary function of children; it is also an important part of a healthy adulthood. In fact, a distinguishing feature of human life is our ability to sustain play throughout our lives. Our uniqueness and, therefore, our purpose is not fulfilled through reason alone. Reason contributes to a distinctive mode of awareness, but more importantly it enables us to sustain creative self-expression, which is most fully realized in play.

For adults and parents in contemporary society, finding the time, energy, and psychological space for play is challenging. Children, on the other hand, seem as though they are born to play. Their energy appears to be limitless while they play. They discover new things about themselves and the world through their desire for adventure, excitement, and surprise. It is through play that children learn who they are and who they can become. As parents we need to work toward providing the appropriate spaces for children to play. These spaces need to be free from danger and from unnecessary restrictions that interfere with the child's desire and need for creative self-expression.

I often marvel at myself and other parents, in that we so often long for children to play creatively, peacefully, and happily, and when they do, we can't resist interrupting and disrupting their play. Children can find such interruptions upsetting, and for good reason. Child-play is not just fun and games. As psychoanalyst Donald Winnicott points out, play serves as a transitional space in which children can bring their subjective desires into contact with the external world though transitional objects and transitional phenomena. In early infancy, for instance, a child may take to thumb sucking as a transition or weaning from the mother's breast. Or in later infancy a child may become attached to a blanket, which he carries around for comfort, warmth, and security. Such transitional objects are essential to the healthy development of children.

One reason these transitional objects are so important is that in early infancy children feel omnipotent. They cry, and food arrives or clothes are changed. The world is magic and they are the magicians. They feel as though they are in control. As children develop, however, their power becomes less predictable, less effective. Parents do not respond with the same degree of attention to the cry of a one-year-old as they do to the cry of a one-month-old. Children begin to learn that they are not omnipotent and that they are distinct from the world. The separation of the child from the mother and the realization that the world is not at his command is a challenging adjustment for a child. Play provides a medium through which these adjustments can be made at a pace that is appropriate for the child. In the transition from infantile omnipotence to childhood acculturation, children adjust by imagining themselves in the roles played by people they see and admire. In playing different character roles, children gain an understanding of how to see things from another's perspective and learn the skills they will use as healthy participants in society at large. Through play children creatively express themselves, and in doing so they learn who they are and who they can become. Play is not only essential for childhood happiness; it is central to the healthy development of children.

Resistance

Just as play is not all fun and games, as I witnessed in the response of my daughters to the birth of their brother, childhood is not all play. For children, childhood is also serious business. We know this because of how forcefully they express themselves and the disdain they feel when their acts of self-expression are not taken seriously. Children are never expressing themselves in a vacuum. The meaning of what they say or do is a function of the context in which they are acting. This context is made up of established norms and expectations of behavior. For the most part, parents are the primary transmitters of these norms and expectations. As children move from the feeling of omnipotence in infancy to childhood acculturation and development, they often interpret the norms and expectations handed down to them by parents as life-denying restrictions. Inevitably the boundaries that parents establish for their children conflict with the forceful, but confused, will of children to express themselves as individuals. As children develop, they do not have a clear idea of who they are. They must learn who they are by interacting with the world into which they are born. But this interaction cannot be one of complete acquiescence. Children need to individuate and express themselves uniquely. That is, they must learn the norms and expectations that are provided to them in accordance with their own cognitive, emotional, and moral development. Some of these norms and expectations will cause little conflict for the child, but others will be questioned, challenged, and trespassed. Hence, resistance is an essential component of a healthy childhood.

Ideally, the boundaries that parents provide are put in place for the benefit of children. By setting appropriate boundaries and enforcing them in an appropriate way, parents provide children with healthy parameters within which and from which they derive the information that shapes their character. These parameters serve as the contextual outlines of who children are, who they can become, and the most effective ways of getting there. But the parameters put in place by parents also curtail the "will to power" of children, their seemingly insatiable desires, and unabashed self-assertion. As a result, children often see parents as life-denying obstacles to get around or resist. In fact, children often demonize parents and wish them gone or at least temporarily out of the way. In the process of separating from parents, children inevitably resist the limits and boundaries that parents provide for them. This is one of the primary points of tension in households, one that often leads to strained relationships between parents and children.

I am convinced that parents could alleviate much of the tension that stems from a child's resistance to parental boundaries by acknowledging and accepting one simple insight: *children are supposed to resist*. Once parents understand that childhood resistance is not only appropriate, but also necessary, behavior, they will realize that their child does not hate them if she does not agree with or gets angry about a parent's position. As a parent, I would be less concerned if my children resisted some of my dictates and guidelines than if he or she complied without question or without resistance. In maintaining an awareness of this necessary function of childhood, parents are less likely to respond to their children with feelings of frustration or anger. Instead, they are in a position to understand the frustration children feel in trying to separate from parents as unique individuals while at the same time being dependent on parents and bound by their guidelines. This type of understanding enables the parent and child to work toward a more civil, rational, and compassionate resolution to conflict.

Understanding that children need to resist in order to form their individuality is not the same as condoning unacceptable behavior, however. I recently brought Caitriona, my four-year-old, to a play date. Before I left she and her friend's older sister engaged in an argument about who would ride her friend's new remote-control car. Apparently, Caitriona had been the last one to ride it earlier in the week. Caitriona disagreed with this account of events and suggested that she would ride it this time and her friend's older sister could ride it after her. Her friend's nine-year-old sister then went into a tirade, pounding and rolling on the floor while screaming that Caitriona was a liar, telling her that she would tell her younger sister not to invite Caitriona next time. Caitriona was hurt and tried to hold back her tears but could not, and she buried her tearful face in my chest.

The nine-year-old was resisting, but her resistance was fueled by a heated anger that seemed disproportionate to the situation. The excessiveness of her anger indicated a deeper frustration than Caitriona's unwillingness to compromise. This deeper frustration was most likely established as a result of enduring circumstances in her life that have built up a deep-seated anger that stews beneath the surface of her everyday personality. The obstacle that Caitriona presented to her was a trigger that ignited this anger. For a nine-year-old child to harbor such intense anger suggests that her feelings have not been adequately expressed, understood, or responded to throughout her childhood development. The boundaries that have been given to her and/or the mode of their implementation need to be adjusted if she is to develop the ability to respond more appropriately to situations in which she is asked to compromise.

Caitriona's eleven-year-old cousin Brighid, who for good reasons is the idol of her younger cousins, was recently reciting playful cheers that she had learned from a movie. One of the rhymes went: "U-G-L-Y you ain't got no alibi." As Caitriona often does, she imitated Brighid and began to recite this cheer. On hearing this, I explained to Caitriona that it was not nice and that it could hurt someone's feelings. A short time later, Caitriona learned another cheer, which she sang for me early one Saturday morning. This cheer was, "I'm naked, I'm raw, but I am definitely not a whore." I was stunned to hear this from my four-year-old, and I knew that I needed to talk to Brighid. I met Brighid a short time later and I heard her reciting the "U-G-L-Y" cheer. I explained to her the same thing I had told Caitriona, and she agreed that the cheer could be hurtful if directed at someone. She enthusiastically followed this cheer with another one, which, according to her, had no bad words. She began to sing the "whore" cheer I had heard Caitriona using. I interrupted her. It was clear from her response that she had no

idea what the cheer meant. On being corrected for the second time, she began to get upset. I quickly explained to her that what she was saying was inappropriate for an eleven-year-old girl, and that even with all of her excellent qualities, she could be misunderstood if people heard her saying it. I
made it clear that I was correcting her out of love and concern for her and
because I wanted her to understand the implications of what she was doing.
As usual, Brighid understood and agreed that it was not something that she
would want to say anymore.

Brighid needed to be made aware of the boundaries that would allow her
to develop herself in the way she wanted to develop. When these boundaries
were presented to her in a rational and caring way, she appreciated them.
Calm and compassionate explanation as a means of providing boundaries is
possible with Brighid because she has cultivated a disposition that is conducive to appropriating those boundaries through mutual understanding. At
the age of eleven she has achieved a high level of maturity, which makes it
easy for her to appropriate reasonable boundaries. She is capable of understanding boundaries through explanation because she has a high level of trust
in those who are guiding her. She has an intuitive understanding of the value
of boundaries because they have facilitated her development into a happy
and well-adjusted child on the verge of adolescence. In other words, her ability to appropriate boundaries is a function of the *ethos* she has developed, for
the most part unconsciously, throughout her childhood.

Habits

In addition to play and resistance, and arising out of play and resistance, is
a third crucial element in the progress of children toward a happy life. This
is the early formation of positive or virtuous habits for living. The word
ethic derives from the Greek word *ethos*, which is often translated as "way
of dwelling" or "habits of being." The task of ethical life is to cultivate an
ethos that is conducive to achieving the good or happy life. Since children
do not have the ability to reflect on their lives and make rational choices,
the habits of being that they develop early on are shaped by their interactions with their parents. For this reason, it is critical for parents to understand and model healthy ethical foundations from the beginning of their
children's life.

Aristotle reminds us of the simple truth that to become good at something we must do that activity repeatedly. One becomes a good builder by
building well and one becomes a good musician by playing music well. Likewise, a person becomes morally virtuous by doing virtuous deeds. Ideally we

act virtuously with enough frequency that our *ethos* or habits for acting become virtuous. The habits on which we act are the basis from which our ethical state of character is formed. A virtuous state of character, or *ethos*, enables us to consistently make appropriate choices in situations throughout life. One reason that morally virtuous people are consistent is that they take great pleasure in doing virtuous deeds. Since virtuous deeds are pleasurable to them, they have an incentive to continue doing them. We know that a deed is virtuous if the pleasures that it produces do not interfere with or detract from one's ultimate pursuit of happiness. For example, we know that the pleasure that accompanies alcohol consumption is not a natural pleasure because, if such consumption becomes a habit, it detracts from one's overall happiness. On the other hand, if one has acquired the virtue of temperance, for instance, she will not overreact to any situation and is likely to find an appropriate response in most cases. The temperate person will consistently act on that virtue because it is pleasurable to do so and it does not conflict with the overall pursuit of happiness. There is no hangover from being temperate. The pleasures derived from virtuous deeds, according to Aristotle, are natural pleasures.

Early childhood is a critical time for establishing an *ethos* or state of character that is conducive to living a happy life as an adult. Lacking the ability to rationally consider options or choices of behavior, children develop the building blocks of their character unconsciously by imitating those who care for them. Hence, manners and politeness are essential for children to learn as a basis for developing healthy habits for living well. By learning manners and politeness, children act virtuously before they know they are acting virtuously. Politeness is a necessary precursor to virtue in children. The unconscious personality traits that they acquire as a result of their childhood interactions with their parents or caretakers determine the appetites they will want to pursue as adults. A child who is exposed to adults who joyfully practice and benefit from virtuous activities is likely to acquire a natural affinity for such activities and the pleasures they provide in adulthood. For such a child, the task of developing a morally virtuous character as an adult, when the faculty of reason becomes active, is less difficult than it is for one who has not been exposed to virtuous activity or virtuous adults as a child. When reason develops the ability to choose behavior, it either confirms or resists the instinctive inclinations that were established in childhood. That is, reason must decide whether or not the pleasures an individual wants to pursue are conducive to a happy life. If one has built up an instinctual affinity for unnatural or unhealthy pleasures, reason will have to resist the urge or impulse that the appetites express. On the other hand, if one has acquired an affinity for the healthy pleasures early in life, reason does not have to resist these appetites. Reason merely has to affirm them, which is a much less strenuous task.

Aristotle and the Thief

Early in my teaching career, I thought that Aristotle was too conservative in his account of an adult's (in)ability to choose the moral life. As a teacher I believe that education is a powerful tool for change. I believe this because my education initiated a major life change for me. On being exposed to great ideas and seeing the energy and enthusiasm of professors who lived a virtuous and joyful life of the mind, I was inspired to pursue a similar path. Despite the difficulty of staying on a path that feeds on intellectual and moral virtue, I recognize the benefits of such a life.

A few years ago I had an experience that tempered my optimism concerning the power of education to change someone who lacks the necessary childhood experiences for shaping a virtuous character. This experience forced me to reconsider my opinion that Aristotle's insistence on getting the *ethos* right from the beginning was too conservative. I was doing some work in my father-in-law's backyard. One of the numerous times I walked across the yard that day, I saw a young man walk up the street, but paid little attention to him. A short time later my father-in-law returned and drove his car into the garage, which opened onto the street. He asked me if I saw his bicycle; I didn't. Being a retired New York City detective, he immediately concluded that it had been stolen. After a couple of minutes of wondering what could have happened, I remembered the young man walking up the street. I told my father-in-law about him, and he immediately set out to find him. Although I had no experience in police work, I knew the neighborhood well, and I had an idea of where the young man may have come from. I followed my hunch and crossed over the bridge that separates my father-in-law's neighborhood from a more volatile Bronx neighborhood. As I drove down White Plains Road, I spotted the young man turning the corner on the bicycle. I was certain it was my father-in-law's bicycle because my wife and I had given it too him as a Christmas gift. I must admit, when I saw the young man riding the stolen bicycle, I had a slight rush of adrenalin. I drove as close as I could to the thief until I could park my car. I jumped out of the car and ran in front of the bicycle, standing over the front wheel. Thinking the thief would be shocked and somewhat reticent having been caught red-handed, I became frustrated—well honestly, I became livid—when he denied that he had stolen the bicycle and treated me as little more than an inconvenience to his day. Since he was unwilling to admit that he had stolen the bicycle and refused to dismount and return it, I glared into his eyes and let him know in language I thought might be easier for him to comprehend that it would be in his best interest to relinquish the bicycle. Finally, I ushered him off of the bicycle. My heart was pumping too fast as I watched him calmly saunter down the street as if nothing unusual had occurred.

I happened to be teaching Aristotle's *Ethics* in class the following week, which forced me to consider Aristotle's wisdom anew. I came to the passage in book 2, section 1, that reads, "It makes no small difference, then, whether we form habits of one kind or of another from our very youth; it makes a very great difference, or rather *all* the difference." A couple of pages later, in book 2, section 3, Aristotle reiterates this idea by quoting his teacher Plato, who writes, "Hence we ought to have been brought up in a particular way from our very youth so as both to delight in and to be pained by the things we ought; this is the right education."[1] I thought about the young man on the bicycle, who seemed utterly indifferent, not only to stealing, but also to being caught. It seemed clear that this event had little or no effect on his character and that he would probably find himself engaging in unwise or immoral behavior in the future. I then imagined what he had been exposed to as a young child and the guidance he had received as he was developing an affinity for those things that would attract him. The *ethos* he had established was leading him to be attracted to the pleasures of a self-destructive path, and he seemed unable or unwilling to recognize this fact. Likely to never have been exposed to healthy boundaries or examples of virtue and its benefits, this young man had developed habits of behavior and of thinking that would be very difficult to adjust. I imaged him sitting in my philosophy class and realized how difficult it would be to uncover the spark that most of my students were cultivating for a life of moral and intellectual virtue. I imagined the feelings he would have to sort through before he could begin to appreciate the wisdom of great philosophers and of his peers sitting beside him. I guessed that he would be full of self-doubt and suspicion in such a setting and would need to do very difficult and disciplined work to overcome such obstacles to learning and a life a virtue.

Psychologist Erik Erikson reinforces Aristotle's insights into the importance of a good beginning by providing a coherent and detailed account of the stages of development beginning in early infancy and leading up to mature adulthood. At each stage of development an individual is faced with the possibility of developing alternative basic attitudes. In early infancy, for instance, a child learns a basic sense of trust or mistrust of the world and himself. If the parents meet certain basic needs such as comfort, food, tenderness, affection, and love, the infant will learn that the world is a place that can be trusted. On the other hand, if the basic needs of a child are not met at this early stage, it is likely that the world will be experienced as an inhospitable place that cannot be trusted. Recalling the example of the young man who stole the bicycle, one could safely guess that somewhere in his childhood he acquired a basic sense of mistrust toward the world. Somehow, he came to believe that he could not get what he wanted out of life by being honest or just.

Erikson's life cycle reiterates the need to get things right from the start, since each developmental stage builds on what has been established during the previous stage. A child who develops a basic sense of trust during the first stage will have a much easier time becoming autonomous during the second stage. During stage 2, the basic disposition of autonomy is the healthy alternative to shame and doubt, which is the basic attitude a young child who does not trust the world is likely to feel. An autonomous individual is more likely to develop into a child who takes initiative in the early school years, whereas the child who has an inherent sense of shame or doubt will be more inclined to feel guilt about perceived inadequacies. Initiative and guilt are the alternative attitudes that are learned during the third stage of personal development.

As children progress through their developmental stages, their disposition, their *ethos*, is shaped unconsciously. Basic attitudes sink into the child's unconscious as a function of the child's interaction with his environment. As the basis on which one's *ethos* or state of character is formed, these attitudes become the habits of behavior that we learn and use to respond to the world. If we acquire the healthy alternative at each stage of development, we will be developing a habitual disposition that takes pleasure from healthy and virtuous activities. In turn, we will be on the way to laying the foundation for what Aristotle describes as a happy life.

In this chapter we have identified two essential activities of children: play and resistance. Through these activities children pursue adventure and creatively express themselves. These functions enable children to develop and articulate the more primordial habits of behavior that are established from infancy through childhood. Hence we can view the relationship between the unconscious formation of habits and the primary functions of childhood (play and resistance) as similar to the interaction between the hardware of a computer and the software it runs. These habits of behavior, shaped from the earliest days of infancy, make up the "hardware" of the personality, which is carried forth or articulated through the "software" (activities of play and resistance). The "hardware" determines whether play and resistance (the "software") enable a child to fully and creatively express herself, or whether we need to observe a child's play to diagnose developmental problems. As parents we need to take seriously the impact we have on a child's development from the earliest stages and recognize that they are unconsciously appropriating what we say, how we act, and the things to which we are attracted. This unconscious appropriation of a child's environment determines the ways in which a child will experience his world. That is, the habits of behavior established in early childhood play a determining factor in a child's ability to achieve happiness.

Notes

1. Aristotle, *Introduction to Aristotle*, ed. Richard McKeon (New York: Random House, 1947).

CHAPTER THREE

An Ontology of Openness

Ontology is the study of Being. It seeks to understand the essence of things or the fundamental nature of reality, and to uncover the truth about what exists. The scope of ontological inquiries ranges from individual beings such as a person or a thing to the universe as a whole. What these inquiries have in common is that they attempt to bring to light meaning and truths that are ordinarily hidden from our view.

But ontology is more than an intellectual inquiry into the essence of things, because human beings are ontological beings. That means that who we are, our essence as human beings, is formed out of and manifest through our ability to perceive, understand, and relate to the essence of other beings and of reality itself. For the most part, however, these relationships are ontologically forgetful. That is, most of our time and attention is absorbed in the busy details of everyday life. This busyness often forces us to relate to the superficial or nonessential aspects of others and precludes an awareness of the complex and mysterious depths of one's self and of others. In this chapter, we will explore the difference between parent–child relationships that are ontologically forgetful and those that are ontologically attuned.

The Ontological Difference

One of the major contributions that Martin Heidegger makes to the discourse of ontology is his articulation of the difference between an ontic, or everyday, understanding of things and an ontological understanding of things. This difference is known as the ontological difference. In seeking to uncover hidden truths about the essence of beings, ontology tries to recover and maintain an awareness of the ontological difference in our relationships with others. An effective ontology does not provide definitions or answers to describe others. Rather it maintains an awareness of the other's complexity and depth, the difference between her everyday self that is visible on the surface and the more intimate, mysterious, and personal dimensions that recede from the light of day.

This is crucial for parents as they try to nurture the forming personalities of their children. So much of a child's life is mysterious and elusive. Parents need to become comfortable with the spontaneity and unpredictability of a child's life while carefully probing for a deeper understanding of what drives their child, the child's fears and joys, strengths and weaknesses. Understood in this way, good parenting is good ontology. It is a process of bringing to light the hidden, emerging essence of children through healthy, mutually enriching relationships.

Ontology is also a process of recovery, or remembering. It helps us to remember things that are so familiar to us that we tend to forget or overlook them. We rely on an ontological orientation toward beings all the time, though we are rarely aware of it. For example, even though a farmer may not explicitly think about the essence or ontological dimensions of the food he produces, when he reaches for an ear of corn, he does so with an implicit understanding of the type of being the corn is. He knows it is ripe. He knows it will decay if it is not harvested. He knows it is nutritious. He knows these facts about the corn because he also knows on a more unconscious and ontological level that it is a living thing that has come from the ground. He knows that the ground is a part of a complex process in which energy and nutrients are absorbed and released. He also knows that this process is intricately tied to weather patterns over which he has no control.

Even though the farmer may rarely consciously reflect on the complex background that gives rise to and constitutes the essence of his crops, he is always relying on an intuitive understanding of their ontological background. The ontological orientation that the farmer enjoys, his understanding of the nature of food and the complex relationships that make it come to life, shapes the way he relates to his crops. Like the farmer, parents operate with an ontic understanding of their children most often, but never without some intuitive or unconscious grasp of their ontological depths. In deciding what to feed the child, we rely on an understanding of what is good for the organism and what is bad for it. In holding the child and keeping him warm, we intuitively understand that children need to feel safe and loved. In loving the child as the most important part of our lives, we understand that the full meaning of her life is sacred, beyond our comprehension. In all of these ways and many more, we intuitively or unconsciously understand and relate to the ontological depths of children. One of the primary purposes of ontology is to retrieve for the conscious mind the ontological awareness that resides in the depths of consciousness, so that we can appropriate it in a more informed and healthy way.

Developing Perceptual Capacities

In order to heighten our awareness of the difference between an average everyday understanding of children and their ontological depth, we need to develop our perceptual capacities. In every perception there is a contrast between the individual thing on which we focus and the background from which the individual thing stands out. The more intensely we focus on the individual figure, the less prominent the background becomes. For example, in the figure below, one can see either a vase in the center of the image or two faces opposite each other. In order to see it as a vase, the faces must become background. In order to see the image as two faces, the vase shape must become the background.

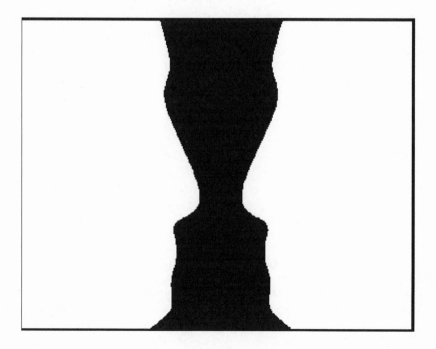

This movement in the perceptual field reveals that beings in their onto-logical depth are dynamic and elusive. These dynamic, hidden, and elusive dimensions preclude our gaining a complete and total picture of others. That is, in their ontological depth, beings cannot be contained within a fixed, conceptual representation of the mind. What we can see and conceptualize always stands out against a background that we do not see and cannot fully represent.

To recognize that it is not possible to have an exhaustive account of a be-ing is a major step toward achieving deeper levels of ontological attunement. Such recognition can initiate a transformation in how we relate to beings. For most of us, we are usually relating with others from an everyday ontic per-spective, in which our primary objective is to get something accomplished. For parents this means getting children dressed, fed, and into the car to go to school. It is getting them into the bath and into bed at a decent hour so they are not exhausted and cranky the next day. We employ different strategies for getting these tasks done.

In relating to children strategically, we tend to see them, or at least some parts of their behavior, as a challenge that must be overcome in order to get things done. While it is necessary to sometimes relate to children in this way, there is a growing tendency to overemphasize the accomplishment of every-day tasks and the strategies that are used to accomplish them. We tend to fo-cus on the task at hand with such intensity that we lose perspective on the relationship as a whole. This is dangerous, because as parents we are en-trusted to facilitate and guide the development of the whole child, not just the routine tasks that we outline for the child. To meet this responsibility, we must become attuned to the ontological depths of our children's lives, even when those depths are difficult to comprehend. Unfortunately, there seems to be a growing trend away from becoming ontologically attuned to our chil-dren. The recent explosion of teenage violence, the widespread sense of alienation among children, and the proliferation of medicated children are symptoms of this trend. Equally tragic is the neglect of our own ontological needs, which must be met if we are to develop as healthy, well-adjusted, and attuned adults. As a first step toward ontological attunement, we must be aware of the danger and the extent of our ontological forgetfulness.

Ontological Forgetfulness

Ontological forgetfulness occurs when we conflate the ontic and the onto-logical, the average everyday understanding of things and the essence of those things, the figure and the background. While such forgetfulness is easily identified in many familiar attitudes and relationships of modern culture, its roots go deep into our philosophical heritage. The guiding assumption of our philosophical tradition has been that there is an answer to the question "What is Being?" and that human rationality can find that answer.

Most of us are aware of the fact that the type of question one asks often shapes the answer that one will receive. The success of trial lawyers, for instance, depends on their ability to ask the right question in the right way. Their questions lead witnesses to give responses that support the case they are trying to make. That is, lawyers shape the perceived reality of a case through the questions they ask. The difference between trial lawyers and philosophers who have traditionally sought an answer to the question "What is Being?" is that philosophers, for the most part, were unaware of the extent to which the question they were asking was shaping the answers they could find. They failed to adequately examine the perspective from which the question is asked. As a result, reason was thought to have a bird's eye—or better, a God's eye—view of reality. That is, philosophers became intoxicated with the powers of reason and paid inadequate attention to the faculties of perception. In overlooking the dynamic, playful, and elusive nature of beings, they incorrectly assumed that an exhaustive account of reality could be achieved through rational representations of Being or reality. In trying to give a coherent description of the world, they forgot about reality.

The desire for coherence, predictability, and clarity is strong in most adults. This desire presents a special challenge to parents, since incoherence, unpredictability, and mystery make up much of childhood. If this adult desire is too strong, it can lead parents to stunt the healthy development of children by neglecting or even denying that which cannot be controlled.

Manipulating Children

One of the most controversial issues surrounding the relationship between adults and children in the United States today is the diagnosis of Attention Deficit Disorder (ADD) or Attention Deficit and Hyperactivity Disorder (ADHD) and the pharmaceutical drugs used to treat them. An estimated six to eight million children are currently taking Ritalin or similar drugs, such as Aderoll, to treat these conditions. I recently watched a documentary telling the story of three children diagnosed with ADHD. The film depicted the experience of the children and their families before and after using the drugs. I was struck by the story of one child who was five years old. He was clearly an active child who seemed to enjoy a high level of physical dexterity. At one point he was shown sliding down a flight of carpeted stairs on his belly at great speed; he hopped up when he reached the bottom with a smile that exuded a sense of accomplishment and confidence. He was then shown moving around his classroom peering at the different projects his classmates were working on, never staying for very long at any one station. His teacher commented on this tendency as an example of his inability to concentrate. While moving around the room, he was very gentle with the other students. He did not touch anything the other children were working on, and if he did touch other children it was gentle and affectionate.

My sense was that the footage of the boy was intended to demonstrate his condition. What impressed me most, however, were the child's parents—in particular, his mother. She resisted the diagnosis and refused to medicate her son. She was not in denial. She understood that her son was energetic and active. But she loved this part of his personality. She did not want to stifle his enthusiasm for life, his curiosity and physical dexterity. She was willing to embrace this enthusiasm and all of its ramifications. But she was faced with a difficult problem. While she saw her son's personality as a gift rather than a disorder that should be medicated, her son's teacher felt that he was too disruptive to the class. From the teacher's point of view, the boy was interfering with classroom procedure and hence with her ability to educate the other students in the class.

Both the teacher and the parent are expressing legitimate concerns. The boy may be too energetic for his class and his teacher. The teacher is responsible for educating a number of students and there are standard methods and procedures for doing so. These methods and procedures are designed to help students achieve what we expect of them and what we think they need to be successful as adults. When these methods and procedures are disrupted, we try to eliminate the source of the disruption or find ways to channel it so that it no longer interferes with the goals of the educational process. In this case, since the school could not accommodate the boy, his mother had to search for a school that could. Her motivation for doing so was to preserve and nurture her son's unique personality, rather than suppress or eliminate it.

Usually, our response to children who express themselves in ways that do not conform to methods and procedures of the established system or to the expectations of teachers and parents is to modify their behavior and bring the errant child into the fold. Increasingly, the method for doing so is the use of chemicals such as Ritalin. Many parents and other adults entrusted with caring for our children welcome the use of pharmaceuticals when they help a child to conform to the procedures in place. Ideally, the authorities advise medication not only out of self-interest, but also for what they believe to be the best interest of the child. From their perspective as advocates for the established procedures and goals of education, they assume that the drugs will help him to learn more easily.

There is evidence to suggest that Ritalin may help students to concentrate and cooperate in the short-term, but none to demonstrate long-term behavioral or academic improvement. There are physical side effects linked to the use of Ritalin—such as dysconsia, stunted growth, heart disease, and even cancer—and there is the equally serious, though less recognizable, problem of using drugs as a mechanism to affect the behavior and perceptual capacities of children. Fundamentally, the danger is an ontological one. That is, the use of Ritalin as a weapon to achieve perceptual and behavioral conformity suppresses the child's energetic and spontaneous responses to the world. While those responses may be disruptive to established procedures and even to the expectations of educational protocols, they may not be inappropriate. As my psychologist friend often points out, sadness or depression is often an appropriate response to what a person has experienced. Similarly, a child who does not conform to the procedures in place may be indicating as much about those procedures as he is revealing about himself. A child who is responding to the world with more energy than his peers may perceive things that others cannot. The child is developing and expressing her complex genetic and cultural inheritance in response to what is perceived. If we medicate the unique perceptions and responses of children, we risk dulling their perceptions of and responses to the world. As a result, we learn little from or about their true selves and true potential. If we were to medicate all the children who do not conform to the prevailing educational standards and procedures, or who seem restless and antsy, we would lose great minds and creativity. In fact, if Albert Einstein or Benjamin Franklin were children today, they would be prime candidates for Ritalin. Einstein was so uncomfortable in school as a child that he stopped going. This should give us pause. How many minds with great potential are being lost to the whims of teachers and parents who do not want to do the work required to understand and nurture the whole child, even those parts that are difficult to understand or work with?

The excessive use of Ritalin is a dramatic example of ontological forgetfulness in two decisive ways. First, Ritalin forces children to become ontologically forgetful by cutting them off from the deep and complex dimensions of their personalities. Second, it demonstrates the forgetfulness of adults who want to medicate children so that they conform to the preestablished worldview of adults. While Ritalin is a growing problem, it is merely the surface of a much deeper problem among parents who find themselves compelled to manipulate children. This compulsion is a symptom of ontological amnesia and it is often caused and sustained by the inability or unwillingness of parents to examine, understand, and work through the repressed conflicts of their own childhood. As psychotherapist Alice Miller so powerfully reveals in *The Drama of the Gifted Child*, unless parents become fully aware of the repressed pain they carry from their own childhood experience, they are condemned to repeat what she describes as "cycles of contempt." These cycles are repeated unconsciously, because parents are often unwilling or unable to revisit their own psychological and emotional pain. Instead they pass it on to their children under the guise of discipline.

The reluctance to face past trauma is born out of a number of factors. First, for many of us, we have so successfully suppressed our pain, we are unaware that it exists and that it informs our behavior and our relationships. Second, for those who have some awareness that there is some pain lurking below consciousness, it is difficult to bring that pain into the light of day and suffer through it again. Third, many adults tend to retain an idealized notion of their parents, and they are unwilling to shatter those illusions.

But as long as we fail to face up to these unconscious fears and the pain from which they are generated, we cannot begin to achieve an authentic existence of our own, and are unlikely to treat our children in the way we would like. Unaware that their behavior is often motivated by the hurt they carry from childhood, parents often repeat behavior that hurts their own children. For instance, a parent who was humiliated as a child may harbor an unconscious desire to be in a position of control that allows him to humiliate someone else. Most often, such desires are realized at the expense of children. The unconscious quality of such behavior is a painful but prevalent example of ontological forgetfulness.

One of the central messages we can take from Miller's work is that parents must achieve a high degree of ontological attunement and authenticity in their own lives if they are to avoid inflicting suffering on their children. Whether we are talking about Ritalin or about contradictory messages of success, parents are often unwittingly motivated by their own fears and suppressed pain. This unconscious and suppressed pain causes parents to indirectly search for the fulfillment of their own needs at the expense of addressing the authentic needs of their children. Until parents face their own pain and work through it, they cannot be open to the needs of their children. They remain forgetful of the ontological depths of their children as well as the ontological depths of their own Being.

The background assumption at work in manipulating or medicating the uniqueness and spontaneity out of children is that the prevailing expectations that adults have for our youth are the correct ones. These expectations are often grounded in false ideas about our own lives and the motivations on which we act. If we fail to adequately listen to the authentic needs of children, our expectations and the protocols developed to achieve them will never be challenged. If Ritalin is used as a weapon for obliterating spontaneity for the sake of conformity, we silence the unique background experience of children. We stifle the expression and formation of their singular genetic and cultural inheritance. This amounts to a negation of the ontological difference, which is the difference between the everyday attitudes that are shared and passed on by prevailing social norms and the infinitely rich and complex field of Being, from which beings emerge and in which they find deep meaning and purpose. Used in this way, parental manipulation is a tool or weapon for ensuring ontological forgetfulness. As such, it precludes the possibility of high levels of self-development and fulfillment, which are achieved through ontological attunement and remembrance in the field of Being.

In order for parents to facilitate the healthy expression and assimilation of our children's unique perspectives on the world, we must be capable of maintaining an awareness of the ontological dimension of our lives and of our children's lives. We need to deepen our awareness of the ground from which and in which our lives find meaning and fulfillment, while also attending to the details of everyday life. That is, we need to keep in view the difference between our ontic, or everyday, relationship to the world and the ontological background that unconsciously drives, shapes, and informs that everyday view.

To become healthy adults and to nurture healthy children, we must get beyond the compulsion to control and manipulate. If we manipulate and medicate our children, we reduce their ability to find, develop, and express their deepest selves. We minimize their association with the deepest sources of meaning, which are found in the field of Being as a whole, by failing to address their essential needs and by dulling their capacities of perception. Rather than stifle their exposure to the ontological dimensions of their lives, we need to facilitate such exposure. We can do this by learning to be fully present and attendant to their developmental needs and by helping them to trust in their capacities and perceptions of the world. They can then use these capacities to understand not only the world and what it reveals, but also their own experience as members of the of the human species, of nature, and of the world. This is what parents want for their children. To get there, we need to forge a path of ontological remembrance.

Ontological Remembrance

In discussing ontology and the task of self-development as a process of heightened ontological attunement, it is easy to get lost in the abstract language of Being. But we must remember that in discussing the ontological horizon or the field of Being, we are also referring to the essence or nature of individual beings. In fact, if we want to get an understanding of our own level of ontological attunement, we need to examine our relationship with other individuals and with the specifics of our own lives. It is in our relationships with the particulars of life that we have access to the ontological dimension of experience. By maintaining an awareness of the particulars, along with the background from which they emerge and within which they have their deepest meaning, we preserve the ontological difference. That is, in becoming ontologically attuned, we are cognizant of the particular and the universal, the individual and its essence, without sacrificing one for the sake of the other.

In our discussion of the importance of ontological remembrance, it is implied that there is something that has been forgotten. Ontological forgetfulness seems to be almost universal among those of us who are products of the Western process of socialization. (We will examine this process in the next chapter.) But what is it that we have forgotten, and when did we know it? The great American poet Walt Whitman beautifully describes the experience of ontological attunement that children enjoy as a natural part of their experience with the world. In the poem "There Was a Child Went Forth," Whitman reveals how intimately children experience the world. He writes,

> There was a child went forth every day,
> And the first object he looked upon and received with wonder or
>   pity or love or dread, that object he became,
> And that object became a part of him for the day or a certain part
>   of the day . . . or for many years or stretching cycles of
>   years.[1]

Whitman describes the malleable and playful perceptual abilities of children to receive that which they encounter with such intimacy and feeling that what they perceive becomes a part of them. These experiences stay with children, sometimes for a lifetime. For many of us, these childhood memories come streaming back to consciousness when prompted by something as simple as a smell, a sound, or a new season. They are often accompanied by the same feelings that occurred with the original event. The endurance of such experiences in our memories reveals how connected we are with the world. As Whitman points out, the child becomes the object, and the object becomes the child.

Whitman's poetic insight foreshadows one of the central insights of Maurice Merleau-Ponty, the twentieth-century French phenomenologist. Merleau-Ponty described the intimacy between human beings and the world in which we live as an intertwining. The same matter that constitutes the flesh of the world also constitutes the flesh of the human body. We are a part of the same process, made of the same matter. But we do not just exist side by side with other things in the world. Our relationship with the world is so intimate that we are a part of the world, and the world is a part of us. We are intertwined with the world and beings in the world. The paradigmatic instance of such intertwining is the mother and fetus. They transmit matter to each other and with it life. This intertwining is transformed, expanded, and deepened by the birth experience. From the beginning, we are intertwined in relationships. In fact, we are made for relationships, not just with human beings, but with the world in which we live. Through the nose, mouth, and ears, the world penetrates and nourishes us with air, food, and sounds. Who we are is a direct function of how we relate to the world: hence the importance of being ontologically attuned to the world in which we live.

It is this openness to the world and the intimacy it makes possible that we tend to forget as we become more entrenched in strategic and manipulative relationships based on calculative reason. It is this intimacy and openness that we want to retrieve if we are to experience and enjoy the world in all of its depths. As parents we want our children to gain confidence in their ability to perceive the world with such intimacy. It is in the processes of socialization, in which instrumental reason becomes the predominant mode of access to the world, that we lose the intimacy and the attunement we experienced as children. Through ontological remembrance, we can recover the experience of enchantment that is so familiar to childhood by expanding and deepening our awareness and participation in the event of Being.

We participate in the processes of Being in many ways. Two of the most prominent modes of participation occur through our genetic and cultural inheritance. These inherited bodies of wisdom provide the tools with which we relate to the world. By opening to and appropriating the ontological background, we deepen our connection to the processes of Being. Nobel prize–winning poet Seamus Heaney provides an example of such openness in a poem entitled "Digging." In this poem Heaney describes the transmission and transformation of ancestral wisdom passed on from father to son. Here are a few excerpts:

> Between my finger and my thumb
> The squat pen rests; snug as a gun.
> Under my window, a clean rasping sound
> When the spade sinks into gravelly ground:
> My father, digging.
> . . .
> By God, the old man could handle a spade.
> Just like his old man.
> . . .
> Between my finger and my thumb
> the squat pen rests.
> I'll dig with it.[2]

Although Heaney is using a pen and not the spade of his father and grandfather, he sees his vocation as a poet through the work of his father and grandfather. He too is digging. Just as they dug the soil, bringing it to life, Heaney digs into the universe of language, bringing it to life.

While poets like Whitman and Heaney give us moving descriptions of ontological attunement, we should realize that such attunement is not limited to the poets. Remembering the ontological difference occurs through the particulars of life. For instance, a gardener is likely to be attuned to nature as a result of growing his own food. He is aware of the relationships among the many variables involved in the growth of a crop before it arrives on the dining table. These variables, such as weather, soil, and growing seasons, are vague background issues for most grocery store consumers. As a result, those of us who shop in the grocery store are less likely to be attuned to the essence of food, and food is not likely to be an item through which we achieve a high level of ontological attunement to the processes of nature. This has important ramifications. As most parents know, it is difficult to get children to eat the proper foods. When we eat processed foods or foods that have been treated with carcinogenic chemicals, we are interfering with the natural processes of Being. These derivative food products diminish the ability of nature to provide nourishment. For those who are ontologically attuned to their bodies and the foods they eat, energy is appropriated more efficiently, and they are more likely to experience high levels of health. So while ontology may sound abstract, ontological attunement is achieved in the practical affairs of everyday life.

Tell Me Something Practical . . .
What Ontology Can Do for Parents

During a recent visit to our pediatrician, Mark, I spotted Joseph Pearce's classic work *Magical Child* on the shelf. When I asked Mark what he thought of Pearce's book, he responded with a tinge of sarcasm, "Tell me something practical." As I draw toward the conclusion of this chapter, I suspect that the reader may have similar sentiments. What can parents take from a chapter about ontology that will inform and improve day-to-day relationships with their children?

The primary benefit of delving into a recovery of the ontological dimension of our own lives and the lives of our children is the recognition that children are intimately attuned to Being, and that they are deep and complex beings who cannot be controlled as instruments. Ontological awareness is accompanied by a shift from a controlling and grasping approach with others to a more open, welcoming, and understanding approach. Ontology makes us realize how limited our perspective is in relation to the vast and complex event of life, including the lives of our children. By opening the faculty of perception to the ontological dimension of our lives and the lives of our children, we release ourselves from the tensions that arise in unreflective relationships with our children. Awareness of the ontological dimension provides a space in which the tension and frustration of everyday life do not easily take hold of consciousness. As we will explore in the next chapter, these frustrations and tensions usually stem from the unmet expectations of the ego-self, which are most often shaped by the expectations of the average, everyday, ontologically forgetful social standards. These expectations, and the practices we engage in to meet them, usually fail to address the fundamental human need to constantly find deeper meaning and purpose in life. This can only be achieved by exploring the ontological dimension of life.

To remain open to the ontological dimension in relationships with our children is a constant challenge. Children often test the limits of their parents' patience and understanding. But, as we pointed out in chapter 2, children must resist parents if they are to define who they are as individuals. In remaining vigilantly aware of the ontological dimensions of our own experience and that of our children, we are not as susceptible to impulsive responses that usually do more harm than good. This awareness also provides us with a clearer vision of the standards by which we want to live and that we want to teach our children to uphold. Because ontologically attuned parents are aware of the awesome potential of children, whose genetic and cultural inheritance carries the distilled wisdom of generations of natural and human experimentation and refinement, their standards for behavior and development are higher than accepted social standards.

The openness required to achieve ontological attunement is akin to spiritual practice. It requires a parent to remain present to himself and to the child in each situation. That is, we want to be aware of the feelings, moods, and emotions that are shaping our behavior when we respond to the child. We want to remember that there are always hidden factors at work in how we relate to children, as there are in how children behave.

I recently caught myself on the verge of making an inappropriate response to my oldest daughter for taking something from her sister. I was sitting down to write when Caitriona charged after her younger sister, Anna, to retrieve a doll. Even though it was a doll that Caitriona rarely, if ever, played with, she was upset. She swiped the doll from Anna and in the process knocked her to the floor. My first reaction was anger toward Caitriona. I began to yell at her. To grab something so forcefully from her sister as to knock her down is unacceptable behavior, and she needs to know that. I quickly caught myself, however. I realized that Caitriona was upset not because she wanted the doll. She was probably upset because she felt as though Anna was infringing on her personal space. These feelings had intensified since the birth of their brother three months earlier. Caitriona needed to be reprimanded for her behavior, but she also needed to know that I understood her feelings. When I went into the room, I told her that I understand how hard it is to have younger siblings taking her things and to have less time with Mommy and Daddy because of the baby. But she still has to use words and not force to settle disagreements. She responded by telling me that she has been using her words but Anna never listens. I hadn't thought about this, but it was accurate, and so I learned about another source of her frustration. When I told her this, she immediately calmed down. A few minutes later, she and Anna were playing together.

Because I affirmed Caitriona's feelings, she felt as though she was understood. In being understood, she was able to find space to step back from her feelings of anger and frustration. Her feelings were arising from her own intuitive understanding of justice and her need to have that understanding recognized. Like almost all young children whose natural development has not been damaged, Caitriona is ontologically attuned. As Whitman reveals in his poem cited earlier, the perceptions of children are colored with intense feelings. These feelings often generate passionate responses. These perceptions and responses are working their way into and out of children's unconscious, prereflective understanding of the world. Children need to know that their feelings are not wrong or bad. Once they are confident that what they feel is legitimate, the feelings through which they experience the world can become a foundation for healthy development. Children thereby deepen their ontological attunement to the world and to themselves.

If I had responded to Caitriona by simply yelling at her for her inappropriate response to Anna, her frustration would likely have deepened. She would have felt misunderstood and perhaps isolated. It would have denied her the opportunity to express her feelings and the source of her frustrations. Such a denial would likely have caused her to doubt the legitimacy of her feelings. For children, this is a critical issue. If we are open to the ontological background of a child's experience, and affirm that experience, they will come to trust in what they feel and in their perspective on the world. As Erik Erikson points out, trust is the primary building block to a healthy personality. By trusting in their own experiences and by having the opportunity to articulate those experiences, children enhance their attunement to the ontological horizon of their own being. In this horizon, they find the resources and the meaning they need to become fulfilled human beings.

Remaining open to the other requires us to develop beyond the self-interested tendencies of the ego-self. Such development is the task of a lifetime, and it is hard work. Now that we know *what* we can accomplish by remembering ourselves in the ontological horizon of Being, and by keeping the ontological difference in focus, we can turn our attention to *how* such development progresses. To articulate just one facet of this type of development, the next chapter will focus on one of the most important skills we must have as parents: listening.

Notes

1. Walt Whitman, "There Was a Child Went Forth," in *Leaves of Grass* (New York: Barnes and Noble, 1993), 305.

2. Seamus Heaney, "Digging," in *Death of a Naturalist* (Boston: Faber and Faber, 1966), 13.

CHAPTER FOUR

Listen, Learn, Lead

Approximately two weeks before my wife gave birth to our third child, we received a phone call from our four-year-old daughter's teacher, Marcia. Marcia was concerned about Caitriona. She noticed that Caitriona's behavior had changed over the previous weeks. She seemed preoccupied, quieter, and less enthusiastic than usual. Marcia wanted to know if anything was different at home. One thing that we noticed was Caitriona's increased fussiness when it came to choosing clothes to wear to school. Even though she picked out the clothes she would wear the night before, she repeatedly changed her mind the next morning and vehemently protested when we finally had to decide for her. After Marcia's call, it became clear that something other than Caitriona's choice of clothes was bothering her. We needed to talk to her to find a way to uncover the source of her anxiety.

We thought that she might be upset about the prospect of being displaced by the arrival of a new baby in the home. She had gone through that process once before with the birth of her younger sister. Perhaps she was remembering and anticipating those feelings. At dinner the next evening, we began our conversation by reminding her of how special she is to us and how much fun it would be to have a new baby in the family. She seemed only mildly interested in hearing about how special she is, but welcomed the opportunity to talk about the imminent birth. We quickly discovered that the birth was the source of her concern, but not because she was worried about being displaced. She was worried about her mother. It seems Caitriona had been listening to the stories of childbirth that had been shared among the adults in her life. Apparently, the stories that influenced her most had to do with cesarean section births. Caitriona began to cry as she told us that she was scared for Mommy because she might have to get her stomach cut open to get the baby out. My wife and I looked at each other on the verge of tears as we realized that Caitriona wasn't worried about herself; she was worried about the health of her mother. We told her that Mommy would not have to have a cesarean section. She and her sister had been born naturally and the third baby would likely be born the same way. She was visibly relieved by this information and quickly recovered her usual sense of curiosity, which prompted her to ask, "How does the baby get out?" We told her, and she was back to her bright and cheerful self almost immediately. Marcia confirmed that there was a significant change in her disposition at school.

We are fortunate to have our children in school at the Early Childhood Center at Sarah Lawrence College. Caitriona's teacher, Marcia, was keenly attuned to her personality. Without receiving any obvious signs that Caitriona was bothered by something, she did notice a change in her disposition and helped us uncover the source of her consternation. When we gave Caitriona an opportunity to express her concerns, they were no longer a burden. Caitriona overcame her anxiety because she was heard. Marcia observed the ruminations of a problem, and by informing us about it she helped us to be better parents. She directed our attention beyond the fussiness about clothes and helped us to listen to what was really bothering Caitriona. As a result, Caitriona became free to resume her full participation at school.

If Caitriona had not had the opportunity to be heard and understood, her experience in school and at home and her experience of the birth of her brother would have been compromised. As I reflect on the interaction between Caitriona and her teacher, I think of the words of philosopher David Michael Levin, who writes, "in listening to others, we allow them to become the person that he or she most wants to be."[1] Helping our children become the people they want to be is perhaps the primary task of parenting. To meet that task, we need to develop the ability to listen well.

Listening as Capacity

We rarely reflect on our ability to listen. We usually assume that if we are fortunate enough not be deaf, we can listen. Listening, for the most part, is pragmatic. It is used as a tool for communication. If we have a problem with listening, we tend to think about how to fix it in medical terms. That is, we might begin to reflect on physiological descriptions of hearing, or biological representations of the ear, as we try to identify the source of the problem. For the most part, however, our understanding of hearing is limited to nonreflective common sense or to medicine and biology.

But if listening is accurately described as a capacity, there is more to it than these two accounts suggest. As a capacity, it has the potential to be developed and used well or to be neglected and used poorly. We all know poor listeners. In fact, most of us are guilty of poor listening from time to time. Good listening requires discipline, the ability to focus, and a high level of personal development. The development required to be a good listener transcends the confines of the ego-self. So in discussing the capacity of listening, we must also discuss the process of self-development.

As parents we need to be aware of the effects that poor listening can have on our children. If we reflect on the disappointment we feel as adults in trying to express ourselves to a poor listener, we begin to get a sense of what a child must feel like when a parent fails to listen and understand. As adults, we have defenses against poor listeners, such as humor, cynicism, and trivial conversation. These defenses protect us from ridicule, rejection, and embarrassment. Children are quite vulnerable to the negative effects that result from not being heard. It is through the responses that children receive from significant adults in their lives that they gain an understanding of their own worth. If they sense that those they look up to and admire are not interested in what they say, their sense of self will suffer. Therefore, it is crucial that parents do the developmental work that is necessary to become good listeners. This development can be understood as a progression through four stages of listening skill: primary attunement (infancy), ego-logical listening, skillful listening, and hearkening.[2]

Primary Attunement (Infancy)

The first stage of listening development occurs automatically in early infancy. During the first months of life, the infant hears unconsciously. There is little differentiation of sounds by the infant. The infant does not understand itself as a distinct being. She does not yet have the ability to identify specific meanings for the sounds she hears. But the infant's experience of sound is still quite meaningful. Although the infant does not rationally decipher or filter those sounds to accommodate a preconceived idea of what the sounds are supposed to mean, she is affected by sounds that occur within her auditory field. At this early stage of life, the infant can be said to hear with the entire body. Whether it is the sound of the mother's voice or a piece of soothing music, the infant often responds with movements of the body and a widening of the eyes. I observe this often with my infant son. His eyes light up and his arms and legs begin to move when he hears his older sisters or his mother talk to him. I also watch him respond to a piece of music by curling up his body, lifting his arms and legs as the sounds drape over him. The music literally moves him.

Recalling our analysis of ontological openness in the previous chapter, we could say that the infant is attuned to the auditory field of sound. This auditory field is that from which all sounds emanate and into which all sounds return as fading echoes. The meaningful sounds that we decipher as individual listeners are distinguished from this field in the same way that visual perceptions of individual things require a differentiation of the figure and the background from which it emerges. Without the faculty of critical reason or a sense of an individualized self, infants do not differentiate the meaning of individual sounds from the auditory field. For infants, hearing is experienced as a prerational, preconscious attunement to the auditory field of sound.

Infants quickly grow out of this early stage of minimal figure-ground, or sound-ground, differentiation, as they learn the meaning of different words and sounds and the tone and rhythm with which they are communicated. The ability to decipher the meaning of different sounds increases as the child individuates and separates from the auditory field and from others with whom he communicates. The meaning of what the infant hears is increasingly a function of his or her interpretative capacities. The infant's interpretative capacities are a function of the ego-logical self, which constitutes the second stage of listening development.

Ego-Logical Listening

Recently, our two-and-a-half-year-old daughter, Anna, was going through toilet training. Early on in this process there were numerous accidents wherein Anna didn't make it to the toilet on time or didn't remember to try. After a couple of encouraging days during which Anna did use the toilet, she reverted back to "forgetting" or to having "accidents" again. Following one of these incidents, my wife asked Anna what happened and why she didn't use the toilet. Anna turned to my wife, and looking her squarely in the eye said, "Mommy, I can't hear you." So by the age of two, children have developed the ability to choose what they will and will not listen to. Comfortable in her diapers and fearful of change, Anna decided not to hear her mother's words about toilet training. While Anna explicitly told her mother that she did not hear her, adults use more subtle and crafty methods of tuning others out. We do so from within the confines of the ego-self.

The ego-self is that part of the personality that is largely defined by the values and expectations of the external or social world. Reason formulates what one has been told about the self into an identity that carves out a space for itself in the world. The ego-self perceives its success or failure, and its worth, according to its ability to meet social and cultural expectations. These expectations, for the most part, are instilled in the psyche early in life by one's parents, and later are shaped by one's peers.

Unlike the undifferentiated infant, the ego sees himself as a distinct and separate individual. At the ego-logical stage of listening, we structure our auditory relationships with others in terms of subject (I) and object (others). Within this stage, we develop listening abilities to meet the demands of daily life. We decipher what people tell us about everyday concerns such as the weather, the economy, and schools, and we use that information to our best advantage. When we hear information that is useful, we process it more deeply than information we deem not useful. At the ego-logical stage of listening, we exert our will to power, our will to control situations, in a way that is most advantageous to the ego's sense of self. If we did not individuate as an ego-self, and develop the listening skills appropriate to this level of personal development, we could not function in everyday life. We use this type of listening skill to execute basic transactions.

Ego-logical listening is important—necessary, even—but we cannot rely on it alone and still develop as individuals and as parents. That is, if we listen from the self-interested standpoint of the ego exclusively, we cannot hear any depth or real meaning in what others are trying to say. My daughter Caitriona recently told me about the frustration she experienced as a result of not being heard. She was at a sleepover with her cousins, and she told her uncle that she had a "pounding headache." Apparently, the way that she described her malady caused the others to laugh. Her cousins did not intend any malice. It seems they found Caitriona's diction surprising and "cute." The problem was that Caitriona wasn't intending to be cute. She was serious. So she interpreted the laughter as a smear against her. The preconceived notions that her cousins had of her, namely, that she was the youngest, a cute four-year-old, shaped their expectations about what Caitriona would and could say. These expectations did not include the description that Caitriona articulated. As a result, her cousins overlooked the intention of her words. As Caitriona explained to me, "they didn't understand me."

This rather innocent instance of insufficient listening becomes magnified when it develops into patterns of adult communication. For instance, I often find myself listening to my wife just long enough to respond with a concern of my own. She will periodically tell me her frustration in trying to find time to get work done or pay the bills, only to hear me interject with a comment about all the work that I have to do. Like most working parents, I usually do have much to be concerned about. In my better moments, I realize that my concerns need to be put on hold while she is expressing her concerns to me. To hear her concerns as mere triggers to express my own is a good example of poor, ego-logical listening. My effort to overcome this tendency is central to my personal development and to the development of our relationship.

The experience of not being heard is frustrating. If it becomes a pattern in one's life, it can be devastating. As psychotherapist Carl Rogers realized, after many years of listening to people classified as mentally ill, "the continued experience of not being heard, really heard, makes some individuals psychotic."[3] Even in less extreme cases, wherein a person is not "mentally disturbed," we can cause significant disturbance by repeatedly ignoring or misunderstanding what she has to say.

In speaking with others, most often we intuitively know whether or not we are really being heard. In most of our conversations throughout the day, we skim the surface of our interests and concerns. We talk about the latest sports news or the weather, never revealing anything of great importance about ourselves to casual listeners. The level of listening attunement that a person offers to us determines the depth to which we will go in revealing ourselves. On the other hand, as listeners, we often find ourselves steering conversations away from anything that might force us to feel another's emotions. This is often dictated by time constraints. But just as often, it is the result of an unwillingness to open the ego-self to situations that it cannot control or explain away rationally, without emotion or feeling. As ego-logical listeners, we shut down and protect those parts of the self that are most private, intimate, and important to us. We push these vulnerable and sensitive dimensions of our person deep beneath layers of fear, not knowing how they will be received if they are revealed in the light of day.

When we are forced to shut ourselves down in this way, it becomes impossible to express those parts of the self that are most important to us. This is critical in the development of children. If their interests, needs, and concerns are constantly suppressed or ignored, they cannot develop or grow. As parents, we effectively smother and kill those parts of their lives that are most important to their development, when we do not provide a safe harbor for their developing inclinations and concerns to be expressed. They cannot feel that they will be ignored, misunderstood, or ridiculed in discussing those things that are most important to them. In a very real sense, the lack of good listeners in a child's life can destroy her personal growth and the possibility of realizing her potential as a human being. Without others who really hear and understand them, children can never articulate, for themselves or for us, the deep, partially formed, and partially understood dimensions of their lives. They can never know their authentic needs, which are inscribed deep within the psyche.

As important as it is for parents to be good listeners, it is equally important that parents hear themselves, their own needs and aspirations. To embark on a path of healthy personal development we need to listen to the emotional and spiritual needs that reside deep within the soul. It is as important to hear and respond to these needs as it is to hear and respond to the body's calls for food and sleep. Authentic emotional and spiritual needs, along with the work that is required to meet them, cannot be adequately addressed within the confines of the ego-self. In fact, they are threatening to the ego-self, because they are elusive, always changing and developing. If taken seriously, these needs demand that one change and develop with them. The ego-self is resistant to change because change requires a suspension of the ego's desire to control its world. This fear of change often precludes real personal development.

Despite the impediment ego-logical listening presents to healthy personal growth, there is a tendency in modern culture to pay too much attention to the ego-self. The ego-self often pursues its desires, only to find itself creating more desires when they are achieved. This cyclical process is played out entirely within the realm of the ego and its vision of the world. This vision fails to open itself adequately to what is different from itself. It sees itself as separate and isolated from others. To achieve personal growth and higher levels of human fulfillment, one must be inspired by and pursue what is new and different. That is, one must go beyond the self-generated boundaries of the ego-logical stage of development.

To overcome this obstacle to change and growth, we need to hear those partially formed and partially understood needs and meanings that lurk below the surface of everyday consciousness and gain some insight into how they affect us and how they affect our children. This requires listening skill that enables one to hear one's own authentic needs and the real needs of children, as well as the companionship of those who have developed listening skill.

Skillful Listening

After the second stage of ego-logical listening, one is in a position to develop listening skill. Skillful listening goes beyond the listening ability that normal living and socialization require of us. In acquiring listening skill, one must have the discipline to silence the idle and distracting chatter that so often commands the attention of the ego-self. The idle chatter of the ego-self prevents us from hearing not only others with whom we communicate, but also ourselves. So the first step in developing listening skill is providing oneself with the silence that is necessary to hear others and to hear oneself.

The silence we procure at this stage of development enables us to make two modifications of ordinary listening that contribute to listening skill. The first modification involves a suspension of our ordinary mode of listening in order to focus on a specific aspect or quality of what we are hearing. For example, a naturalist walking through the forest is more keenly attuned to the distinct sounds of the forest than one who is unfamiliar with such a setting. Whereas the naturalist can distinguish and identify the different bird sounds, the casual visitor hears only bird sounds. The suspension of ordinary listening is a technique that psychotherapists use in order to uncover the conflicted feelings or emotions that lie beneath the client's words. Rather than searching for one overall meaning in what a client is expressing (often there is no single meaning), the attuned therapist listens for significant ideas or expressions that may lead to other important issues of which the client has yet to become aware.

Parents are repeatedly called to be psychotherapists for their children. The emotions and feelings that children experience are often far more complex than their ability to articulate them. They often get frustrated trying to express their emotions and feelings, because words often fail to convey the depth of emotional experience. Parents effectively guide children beyond their frustration by listening for at least one idea that they can help the child to articulate clearly. By working through one idea with the parent, the child overcomes the frustration of not being understood. Adele Faber and Elaine Mazlish, the popular authors of *How to Talk So Your Kids Will Listen, Listen So Your Kids Will Talk*, encourage parents to repeat what the child is telling them or describe what the child is feeling rather than trying to assuage the child with advice or encouragement. This technique is effective because the child gets a sense that the parent is listening and does understand. In this way, the parent has entered their child's universe using the child's terms. From this common ground, parent and child can work toward a clear idea of what the child is trying to say. This is very different from imposing one's view on the child or trying to distract the child from what he is trying to say.

When a child trusts that the parent is really listening and trying to understand, he will usually say more about what he feels. As the child says more about what he feels, he can usually work through his feelings and understand them better. In contrast, if a parent tries to make the child forget about what he is feeling, the child can become more frustrated, feeling as though he is not being heard or understood. As a result, he may feel isolated, as if what he has to say or what he feels is not important. So by suspending our ordinary way of listening, which seeks to identify an overall or general meaning in what is being said, we focus in on one idea, or thought, or feeling that the child is trying to express. In this way we let the child know that we are highly attentive to his words and concerns, even if we do not fully understand what he is trying to express.

The second modification involves letting go of inhibitions that prevent us from hearing another. We all have unconscious inhibitions that have been accumulating throughout our lives. To let go of inhibitions is to open oneself to the other. It involves suspending one's own positions in order to better understand the position of another. For those who have achieved a high level of listening skill, the suspension of inhibitions is not difficult. The story at the beginning of this chapter demonstrates the grace with which a skillful listener can hear what others usually miss. Marcia, an experienced teacher and skillful listener, recognized that something was bothering Caitriona. This did not require a radical suspension of Marcia's beliefs. But it did require openness, sensitivity, and attunement to what Caitriona might be going through. By taking the time to learn what she can about the family lives of her students, Marcia is able to interpret their daily behavior against the background information of their lives outside of the classroom. Marcia knew there was a baby expected in our family, and this background information helped her to understand the specific behavior that Caitriona was manifesting. To put this example in ontological terms, Marcia perceived or heard the ontic behavior of Caitriona (her melancholy) against the ontological background, which consisted of the impending birth and everything else she knew about Caitriona as a result of being with her for six months. A skillful listener hears both the specific sounds that one articulates and the background from which those sounds are differentiated. To hear someone on this level often requires letting go of the ego-self's inhibitions.

There is perhaps nothing more important to one's personal development or to facilitating the personal development of children than skillful listening. For parents, entrusted to provide an environment in which children can flourish, the cultivation of listening skill ought to be a high priority. For parents, the biggest challenge in this process is finding the time and space to hear the silence in which skillful listening is grounded. But this challenge must be met, because it is from this silence that we can begin to identify the inhibitions that might prevent us from adequately hearing our children. This silence provides the space from which we can better understand the background experiences of children and their influence on specific behaviors or ideas that our children express.

Just as important as facilitating the development of our children, listening skill facilitates the personal development of parents. If parents fail to adequately develop some of their own human potential, they will not be able to adequately facilitate the well-being of their children. Listening skill, therefore, is a key element in accomplishing parents' own fulfillment and that of their children. Describing his experience as a psychotherapist, Carl Rogers articulates the urgency of listening skill for both the listener and the one who is heard:

> I believe I know why it is so satisfying to me to hear someone. When I can really hear someone, it puts me in touch with him. It enriches my life. . . . When I really hear someone, it is like listening to the music of the spheres, because, beyond the immediate message of the person, no matter what that might be, there is the universal, the general. . . . When I say that I enjoy hearing someone, I mean, of course, hearing deeply. I mean that I hear the words, the thoughts, the feeling tones, the personal meaning, even the meaning that is below the intent of the speaker. Sometimes in a message which superficially is not very important, I can hear a cry, a deep human cry, a "silent scream," that lies buried and unknown far below the surface of the person.[4]

In this passage, Rogers gives the reader a sense of the satisfaction one can experience as a result of listening deeply to someone. In listening to another person, we gain access not only to the inner recesses of her soul, but also to the auditory field in which words and feelings find their deepest meaning. But listening skillfully does not just benefit the listener. Rogers gives us some insight into what it means to be heard by a skillful listener:

> When I do truly hear a person and the meanings that are important to him at that moment, . . . many things happen. There is first of all a grateful look. He feels released. He wants to tell me more about his world. He surges forth in a new sense of freedom. . . . The more deeply I can hear the meanings of this person, the more there is that happens. One thing I have come to look upon as almost universal is that when a person realizes he has been deeply heard . . . in some real sense he is weeping for joy. It is as though he were saying, "Thank God someone has heard me. Someone knows what it is like to be me." In such moments I have had the fantasy of a prisoner in a dungeon, tapping out day after day, "Does anybody hear me? Is there anybody out there?" And finally, one day, he hears some faint tappings which spell out "Yes." By that one simple response he is released from his loneliness; he has become a human being again.[5]

Through his experience as a clinical psychologist, Rogers came to realize that in listening to others, and hearing the depths of what they say, we help them to listen to themselves. As skillful listeners we provide the safe harbor for others to reveal what is most important, most vulnerable, and most sensitive about them. In doing so, we help them to become more the person they want to be, because most often these deep and complex dimensions of life are unclear and confused. We are not sure what they mean or how they affect our lives until we have a chance to express them to a sympathetic ear. This leads philosopher David Michael Levin to write, "in listening to others we help them to become the human being he or she most wants to be. . . . In listening to the sounds of nature, listening to the music of sounds, and listening to the speech of others we learn, we grow, we help others to learn and grow, and we realize that our hearing is a gift to be valued and enjoyed."[6]

For parents, developing the skill of listening will not only improve the lives of their children, it will provide them with a means for enjoying their own lives. As Rogers points out, it is rewarding to really hear what someone has to say. We connect with people on a level that is not accessible in everyday conversation. By connecting with others, we enrich our own lives. If Rogers can have this experience with strangers, imagine the joy that is available to parents who learn to connect with their children through listening skill.

Hearkening

Listening skill is achieved at the third level of personal development. It is difficult to achieve because of many temptations and obstacles we face at the ego-logical stage of listening. Listening skill is a practice of the self that requires discipline and perseverance in stepping back from the persistent chatter of everyday communication. As difficult as it is to achieve the third stage of listening skill, there is a higher level of listening development that is even more difficult. This is the level of hearkening. Those who achieve the level of hearkening have cultivated a spiritual self that enables them to connect with others in a deeply intimate way. At the level of hearkening, we experience the highest levels of human fulfillment. While this stage is difficult to achieve, I believe that many parents have experienced at least a glimpse of it at some time in their relationships with their children. By freely choosing to develop this level of listening as a practice of the self, we can sustain this level of fulfillment for ourselves and for the benefits it will bestow on our children.

The primary characteristic of hearkening is *gelassenheit*, which is the German word for letting go or letting be. At the fourth level of listening development, the confines of the ego-self no longer impose themselves on the ex-

perience of listening. The separation between the ego-self and others and between the ego-self and the auditory field that occurs at the second stage is
overcome. In effect, what transpires at the level of hearkening is a reversal of
the figure-ground differentiation that was achieved at the second and third
levels of listening. In other words, we reconnect with the auditory field of
sound in a way that is similar to the prerational attunement that we experienced as infants. The major difference between the primal attunement of infancy and hearkening is that the latter involves conscious awareness of the
auditory field in which and to which we are attuned. We become completely
open, welcoming the sounds that come our way without judgment or critique. Unlike in the third stage, we do not even attempt to interpret the profound meanings that reside beneath the surface of sounds. At the level of
hearkening, we surpass the abilities of reason to provide meaning to our experience. We are connected with and immersed in the deepest recesses of
meaning, where our life finds its greatest fulfillment.

As an example of this level of listening, I think back to one of the saddest
moments in the life of the community in which I grew up. Over the span of
three short months, we endured three tragic deaths. Our community is geo-
graphically defined as approximately one square mile by a wood, a cemetery,
and a parkway. There are few unfamiliar faces and many lifelong friendships.
While all of these deaths were tragic, the first was the most shocking. Our
friend was in his midtwenties. He was engaged to be married in May to his
high school sweetheart, also a lifelong friend of many in the neighborhood.
In January, on his way home from a ski trip, he fell off of a bus traveling at
full speed on a highway. He died instantly. As with all such tragedies, this one
was inexplicable, and the pain left behind was almost unbearable.

One of the things that struck me about that tragic event was the maturity
of the response that most people displayed during the mourning process that
followed. While wakes are always uncomfortable times for those who come
to pay their respects, this one was particularly sad. There was nothing anyone could say to make the situation any lighter. But nobody tried. Instead,
people embraced silence and listened. They offered their shoulders to be
cried on, while trying to hold back tears of their own. Each person, in his or
her own way, was living the advice St. Francis of Assisi, who prayed to God
to make him a vehicle of peace: to seek not to be consoled, but to console,
not to be understood but to understand, not to be loved but to love. Each
person understood intuitively that words of consolation were ineffective, inappropriate even, but silence and listening were real. The family and fiancée
of the deceased, who suffered the deepest pain, understood that those who
were willing to listen felt their pain with them. In knowing this, they also

knew they were not alone. In feeling one another's pain, there was an intimacy, a connection, that may have offered some small comfort that could not be found anywhere else or in any other way.

In this tragic event, communication occurred not through words, primarily, but through feelings. Just as the infant hears with the entire body, the pain and concern that was shared among our community was communicated through feelings. People felt one another's pain; they did not try to avoid it or eliminate it. The pain of a tragic event shattered the ego-logical interests of an entire community, opening its members to the depths of meaning and of Being, which, in this case, was not a joyful place to be.

We do not want to rely on tragic events to realize the potential we have for human fulfillment and connectedness with others, especially our children. I use this example to demonstrate the intimate connections we can share with others through hearkening. We are capable of listening with and through feelings and emotions rather than with the self-interested ego. But we need to cultivate this capacity so that it is a part of our character and not left to chance. As parents, we want to be able to connect with our children by really hearing them, that is, by feeling their pain and their joy with them. We want to be more than casual spectators of the events of our children's lives. They need to know that we feel their joy and their pain with them. We need to experience the satisfaction of their joy when they ride their bicycle for the first time or their sadness on losing a close friend. Such witnessing is what makes children understand the significance of what they have accomplished and the significance of their lives. Video cameras cannot replace this type of witness, because children feel us feeling for and with them. When we open ourselves to this level of intimacy and participate in our children's lives by really listening to them, we create an enduring bond of trust that makes our children comfortable in revealing themselves to us throughout their lives. As a result, we are in a position to guide them more effectively as they navigate the turbulent waters from childhood to adulthood.

Listen to Lead

At the third and fourth stages of listening there is a strong emphasis on empathic connections with others. To have an empathic connection requires a diminishment or even an overcoming of the ego's self-interested desires. Some may feel uneasy in suspending their own positions and allowing themselves to be completely open and vulnerable to the other's position or pain. Whether the other is an adult or a three-year-old, this level of openness may lead some to fear a loss of control or status in the relationship. It may seem that this level of listening demands that one become too passive to effectively guide others. For parents, this is a real concern, because we know that in guiding children we need to set limits to their behavior. Children need to be taught what is acceptable and what is unacceptable. This focus on the passive dimension of skillful listening may seem to point to an undermining of the parent's authority.

While such a response is understandable, it is based on an incomplete understanding of the power of good listening. This power stems from the ability of skillful listeners to hear the truth in a situation. That is, highly developed listeners are in the best position to lead others because they hear the details and the nuances of a situation. They hear the cries of injustice from those who are treated unfairly and who often go unheard. They hear the deception in the voices of those who have something to hide. The skillful listener is in a position to defend her child if he is treated unfairly by a sibling or a friend, because she can hear truth between the lines of a story. But she is equally poised to correct or guide her child when his story fudges the truth or when he is not revealing his true feelings about someone or something. A highly attuned parent can feel the discomfort or fear that leads a child away from the truth and into deception. By hearing this discomfort or fear, a parent can make the child feel comfortable with the truth, even if it is difficult.

Empathic connections with others, including our children, do not preclude strong and decisive decision making and leadership. In fact, the insights that skillful listening and hearkening provide are a prerequisite for the strongest and most convincing leadership a parent can offer. The skillful listener knows that a tired child sometimes needs to be put into bed, not to be coaxed or reasoned with. She knows that when her child is fussing over the color of her nail polish or clothes, there are deeper issues of independence, control, and separation at work. With these insights, highly developed listeners are in a better position to discern what is useful, true, or important than are unskilled listeners.

It is important to remember that listening skill is a practice of the self. It is something we must work on throughout our lives. At the higher stages of listening, parents experience the inner strength and inner calm that enables them to discern the level of engagement that is appropriate in each situation. As most parents are aware, children can bait parents into conflict over issues that seem insignificant in retrospect. The highly developed listener can hear the motivations of a conversation or a comment. She can hear the inner conflict of the child that leads him to say or do something that needs correction. In hearing on this level, a parent has the perspective she needs to avoid engaging in futile conflicts.

One of the biggest challenges in reaching the highest level of listening skill is releasing the self from the control of the ego-self. While the ego-identity is necessary for making our way through the world as individuals, we must resist its powerful grip when it comes to hearing others and ourselves. The self-interestedness of the ego does not allow for the deep and intimate connections that occur at the higher levels of listening development. It is through these connections that the highest levels of human fulfillment are achieved. It is through these connections that parents and their children learn who they are and who they have the potential to become.

Notes

1. David Michael Levin, *The Listening Self* (Boston: Routledge, 1989), 88.
2. For a detailed account of the four stages of listening, see Levin, *The Listening Self*.
3. Carl Rogers, *On Becoming a Person: A Therapist's View of Psychotherapy* (New York: Houghton Mifflin, 1995), 57.
4. Rogers, *On Becoming a Person*, 59.
5. Rogers, *On Becoming a Person*, 70.
6. Levin, *The Listening Self*, 88–89.

CHAPTER FIVE

Enchantment and the Ethos of Education

Parents are not alone in shaping the character of their children. After parents and peers, the most influential factor in the lives of children is or should be their education. It is understandable then that parents spend vast amounts of time and energy thinking about, discussing, and providing for education, from early childhood through college. In choosing a school for our children, we are choosing the environment that is going to both enhance and challenge the values by which we want our children to live. Their peers and teachers at school will exert an influence over them that parents never can. Education has a major impact on family life. As a result, parents must think very carefully about the education of their children.

The choices that we are faced with in providing for our children's education are often clouded by the standards of education in the United States today. Parents need to be aware that measurements of success such as standardized tests and inflated grades can be misleading. Education, as it operates throughout much of the United States, fails to honor the potential our children bring to the classroom. In blindly accepting these standards and the protocols used to meet them, parents and educators also fail to honor the potential of their children. In this chapter, we will examine both the pitfalls and the possibilities of the educational experience as a means of enhancing our success as parents.

Physics at Seven

During our last visit to Ireland, my wife and I enjoyed the privilege of meeting two young families that had emigrated from Germany to county

Kerry. The fathers of the families were brothers: one an electrical engineer and the other a carpenter. They had transformed the land they had bought from a fallow hillside into a flourishing, self-sufficient farm. They grew organic food in the greenhouse they had built and in gardens spread around the property. They made their own cheese and beer. Most impressively, they generated their own solar and hydroelectric power, which was stored in stacks of batteries in the corner of the workshop. At the time that we were visiting, they had just purchased an old fishing vessel that was in disrepair. They have since restored the boat to its original beauty and use it for deep-sea fishing.

Each of the young couples had two children. The oldest was seven. After a tour of their farm and conversations with both the parents and the children, I asked one of the fathers where the seven-year-old boy goes to school. He told me that the boy wasn't in school, and he wasn't sure where, or if, the boy would go to school. I had spoken with the children and I knew they were very bright, especially the seven-year-old. So I probed a bit deeper to learn the father's thinking on the education of his children. To satisfy my interest, he invited the seven-year-old to join our conversation. He began telling me about the rowboat they had built to use on the lake on the top hill of their property. In the process of describing their project to me, the father periodically asked his son to explain the principles of physics that were at work in building a boat and making it work efficiently on water. As the story progressed, I was astonished by the knowledge of this seven-year-old. His command of the basic elements of physics and electromagnetic energy was at a level that most high school graduates never achieve. I realized that what he was describing with such familiarity, passion, and joy was material that I did not encounter until I was ten years older than the boy. How could it be that a seven-year-old had this knowledge when most people, even in highly regarded schools, do not begin to think about it until they are much older?

The father explained that the boy learned the abstract principles of physics only after having witnessed how they work with real objects. He watched the displacement of water and the buoyancy of the boat. He worked on the mill that sends energy to the batteries in which it is stored. By working with these phenomena, the boy had a step-by-step encounter with what the father would then explain to him from a theoretical point of view. The boy learned by doing.

My day with the two German families made a lasting impression on my understanding of education and of parenting. It first caused me to reflect on my own educational experience, which I deplored until college. I thought of the difference between how the seven-year-old boy living in Ireland was learning about the world and how it works and the way we educate children in schools across the United States. Millions of students sit at small desks day after day for hours at a time, listening to a teacher talk about theories, events, and facts abstracted from the world in which children live. Students are expected to shut down their physical interaction with the world and learn almost exclusively with the intellect. It also revealed to me how little parents, in general, participate in the education of their children. Even though most of us do not run an organic farm for a living, there are many projects and hobbies that we can do with children to substantially enhance their education. As my wife and I attempt to chart an educational path for our children, we are both inspired and challenged by the example of the German families in county Kerry. We are inspired to know what children are capable of but challenged to find schools that are honoring that potential.

One way of understanding the mainstream approach to education is to recognize that the long-standing Cartesian view of human nature—which privileges the intellect as the seat of the human soul, while reducing the body to the state of mere obstacle to learning—dominates the modern approach to education. By presupposing this separation between the intellectual and the physical, between the mind and the body, we have artificially dissected our approach to learning. After encountering a seven-year-old who not only has a command of material that most students do not encounter until they are seventeen, but who also has an enchanted, joyful look in his eye when he shares his knowledge with others, one is forced to examine the prevailing trends of education.

In light of the current educational crisis, there are three perspectives on education that parents need to carefully consider. First, we need to examine the expectations we bring to the educational experience. These expectations need to be held in contrast to the second perspective we need to explore, which asks the question, "What *can* we hope for from education?" Here we are concerned with the highest goals and potential of education. These ideals have been largely forgotten or ignored in the familiar, everyday understanding of the purpose of education. Finally, we need to consider some examples of how the highest potential can be achieved through alternative approaches to education.

What Do We Hope For?

I remember trying to decide what I would major in when I went to college. I hadn't given it much thought before getting there, but as the son of Irish immigrants who came to the United States to make a living, I began college with utterly practical concerns. I thought that if I graduated with decent grades in a discipline that was relevant to the mainstream world of commerce and finance, I could find a decent-paying job and live happily ever after. In my sophomore year I declared economics my major. I was on my way to Wall Street. Or so I thought.

I could not have anticipated the life-changing experience of the first philosophy classes I took at Vassar College. Wrestling with the ideas of Plato and Aristotle, and catching the infectious enthusiasm of some of the best professors one could hope to have, I was thrust into the enchanted world of inquiry and self-reflection. I took Socrates seriously when he argued that to care for one's soul is primary, and everything else follows from it. I learned to think logically and critically about the texts we read as well as the information we are fed from the plethora of media outlets that surround us. While reflecting on the great ideas that have been passed on throughout our intellectual history, I had a new sense of freedom and hope that was unlike anything I had ever experienced. I realized that what the philosophers were talking about was not mere information to be memorized and regurgitated on an exam. In an articulate and reasoned manner, they were wrestling with the most important issues of human life, which I quickly realized were the most important issues of my own life. Philosophy is serious business, because it forces us to examine the beliefs according to which we live. It challenges us to become conscious of the ideals we hold and to close the gap between our ideals and our everyday habits of behavior. The effect of those early days in philosophy catapulted me into a life of inquiry and a love of learning. But I remained painfully aware of the practical side of life. I knew I needed to make money. I now had to find a way to make money while also trying to care for my soul.

Most of the students I teach also bring practical concerns and goals to college. Along with their parents, they see education as a means of achieving a higher standard of living. In general, standard of living is measured by one's salary and the things it enables one to purchase and consume. This measurement of standard of living is reinforced by the global expansion of the market economy. To survive in such an environment, one must be cognizant of the need to earn an acceptable wage. For those of us with children, the amount of money we earn is an ever-present challenge, as we search for a suitable place to live, plan their education, and encourage extracurricular activities. All of these things require money. Accordingly, many parents use their education to make themselves marketable employees or professionals in the pursuit of the highest wage possible.

Along with parents and students who are working with this pragmatic conception of education, many educators, and the institutions for which they work, promote this practical approach. As a result, the fields that dominate contemporary education are those that give students the skills that make them marketable in the modern economy. These are the areas that will offer students the highest-paying jobs, which usually have to do with finance, science, and technology. The powerful emphasis that has been thrust on these fields has vital implications for how we live our lives. For instance, in making science the most important discipline, we assume that all knowledge must meet the scientific criteria of truth if it is to be considered valid. By reducing the idea of truth to one type of truth, we eliminate, or cast crippling suspicion on, vast fields of nonscientific knowledge and wisdom that play a crucial role in helping us to understand our place in the world. We cannot scientifically measure emotions, feelings, or moods. Yet, they play an integral role in everything we do. We cannot quantify a parent's love for her child, but it is the most important part of a child's development. The emotional development of a child will shape many of the child's decisions throughout life. It is peculiar then how widely accepted is the underlying assumption that scientific truth is the only form of truth. This assumption holds that the world and nature, as well as our interaction with them, can be known and understood in one way, through the measurements of mathematics and science.

Of course, our experience of the world tells us something very different. When we appreciate the shade of a tree on a hot summer day, there is a visceral intimacy that we share with nature that cannot be measured, just as we cannot measure a parent's love for her child. The feeling of intimacy with nature and the depth and passion of parental love are examples of the type of experiences that give life its richness and meaning. An important part of a good education helps children develop an appreciation and understanding of these kinds of experiences through literature, art, history, and philosophy. It is not enough that we introduce students to computers at ever-younger ages, so that they will be prepared to compete in our technological world. Such policy is founded on a faulty vision of the educational enterprise. But what is this vision? What is the end result that parents, and students who pursue a strictly practical approach to education, envision? To answer these questions, let us glance back at Plato's account of the human soul in his most famous dialogue, the *Republic*.

A large part of Plato's *Republic* is devoted to working out his understanding of justice. To explicate his idea of justice, Plato outlines his vision of the ideal state, which he sees as a magnification of the individual soul. The ideal state and the ideal soul have three distinct but related parts. The state is made up of a ruling class, a military, and the craftspeople and merchants. The soul consists of reason, spiritedness, and appetites. Ideally, for both the state and the individual soul, the three parts work harmoniously together, each one doing its job without interfering with the others. The ruling class is responsible for governing the state by making decisions that will benefit society as a whole. The military is responsible for enforcing those decisions. The craftspeople and merchants are responsible for providing the necessary goods and services the society needs to live well. For the individual soul, reason is responsible for making insightful decisions that are beneficial to the whole person. If the person is healthy, or, as Plato puts it, if the person is a friend to himself, the insightful decisions made by reason are enacted because the other two parts of the soul, spiritedness and appetites, are working with, rather than against, reason. When these three parts of the soul are harmoniously integrated with one another, one has achieved a just soul. If one or more parts of the soul overstep their proper function, the soul becomes imbalanced, and it is an unjust soul. When this happens, the individual is not a friend to himself. In other words, he makes decisions that eventually come back to harm him. His behavior is self-destructive.

The most obvious example of this type of soul is found in the life of drug addiction. When sober, the addict can speak rationally and coherently about what he wants and what he needs to do to achieve his goals. Reason understands what is best for the individual as a whole person, but the appetitive part of the soul interferes with the insights of reason. The addiction or appetite that has forged its way into the cellular and neurological pathways of the organism co-opts the spirited part of the soul, pulling it away from reason. As a result, even though reason knows what to do, the imbalance of the soul leads to self-destructive behavior.

The self-destructiveness of drug addiction is obvious. But there are more subtle forms of self-destructive behavior that Plato's model of the soul can help us to recognize. When we examine the goals of the exclusively practical approach to education, we realize that in many instances, the primary and often the only concern is procuring the assets we need to satisfy the ever-expanding desires of the appetitive part of the soul. Though we may make rational decisions about our daily activities, the forum within which we employ the powers of reason is shaped by the appetitive part of the soul. That is, we spend a disproportionate amount of time and work accumulating spending power, which ultimately is used to address the demands of the bodily appetites. In a sense, we imitate the beasts who spend their days searching for food and shelter and, when in season, a mate to procreate.

But we have the capacity for self-reflective thought. We have the ability to pursue higher ideals. We can change behavior that we find working against us if we become aware of the causes of such behavior. Because we have these abilities, which are born out of the faculty of reason, we cannot be satisfied by a life that is dominated by procuring material goods. Meeting the demands of material life is necessary, but it fails to fully address the emotional, psychological, and spiritual needs of the human organism. Nor can these needs be met by gaining expertise in finance, science, or technology alone. In fact, without the wisdom that is required to uncover the sources of deep meaning and purpose in life, the knowledge, skills, and assets that we acquire are as likely to work against us as for us. Just as the second stage of listening development is necessary for meeting the demands of everyday life, but not sufficient for achieving higher levels of fulfillment, technical know-how and material wealth are also necessary, but they will not guide us to an integrated life of deep meaning, purpose, and joy. Hence, in addition to providing the skills for practical life, education has an urgent responsibility to provide hope for a better future, both individually and collectively. A good education will enable our children to make wise decisions and cultivate relationships based on values that have been refined over centuries of intellectual, spiritual, historical, and natural evolution.

What *Can* We Hope For?

One way of understanding the current crisis in education is to recall the ontological difference we discussed in chapter 3. This is the difference between the ontic, everyday dimension of human experience and the ontological dimension, which consists of the deeper experience of Being (the emerging essence of all that exists in the world), and of one's essence as a person. The ontological dimension transcends the details of everyday life but also provides the ground in which those details have their deepest meaning. Unfortunately, the ontological dimension is often overshadowed or forgotten in the busyness of everyday life. When this happens, we engage in a futile search for meaning in the ontic domain, with the inevitable result of feeling frustrated or empty. Human life cannot find deep meaning or purpose without incorporating the ontological depths into experience. Whatever we achieve in the ontic realm, as individuals or as a species, will only work toward our well-being if it is understood in relation to the ontological. Education ought to be a medium for integrating ontic, everyday experiences with the ontological, which provides our lives with deep meaning and purpose.

The current trends in education, however, seem to suggest that education has become a tool for ontological forgetfulness, rather than a means for appropriating the ontological dimension in everyday experience. For instance, we currently spend billions of dollars on education in the United States, while we make standardized testing a national priority. By overemphasizing standardized testing we undermine the educational process, because teachers and administrators are forced to prepare their students for exams rather than encourage them to think critically and creatively. The learning process becomes laden with the pressures to pass exams rather than the joy and enchantment of discovering, reflecting on, and understanding new knowledge. In this type of setting, too many students experience education as a burden, whereas the seven-year-old German boy I met in Ireland radiated with enthusiasm when speaking about the mathematics and physics he learned while building a boat. The German boy is acquiring knowledge by integrating his experience of the world with his father's knowledgeable explanations of that experience. In his work with the elements of nature to sustain and enhance the lifestyle of his family, mathematics and physics take on deep meaning and relevance for him. In contrast, when exams are the primary reason for learning and the only outlet for expressing knowledge, students have a difficult time integrating their academic knowledge with their everyday lives. As a result, what they learn in the classroom has little relevance to them outside of the classroom. One of the primary tasks of education is to render knowledge relevant to the lives of students.

Aristotle begins his *Metaphysics* with the statement that "all men, by nature, desire to know." We have an innate curiosity for knowledge. When that curiosity is fed in the appropriate ways, it grows. Another essential function of elementary education, therefore, is to cultivate this innate curiosity into a love for the learning process. This love is the *ethos* that the best type of education cultivates in students. Of course, such an *ethos* demands that children gain a command of the basic tools of learning: reading, writing, and arithmetic. Without these tools, it is difficult for a child to learn and therefore difficult to love learning. The excellent elementary school teachers I have met give students a command of the basics by exposing them to the world in which they live. They learn to read, write, add, and subtract by studying a bird habitat outside of their classroom window or traveling to local parks and streams to gather data, which they weave into a story about the health of the natural environment in which they live and play. They see, touch, feel, and hear what they are studying, making letters, words, and numbers come alive. This is essential in establishing a love of learning, the enchanted *ethos* of an excellent education.

In Plato's *Apology* we find one of Socrates' most famous lines of wisdom, "the unexamined life is not worth living." Socrates spent his life exhorting his fellow citizens to examine their own lives so that they would be clear and honest about how they lived and who they were. He was challenging them to know themselves better, because without this knowledge, life is severely compromised. In addition to making education more relevant to the lives of children and nurturing their innate curiosity, a third essential element in a complete education is the cultivation of an ability and willingness to continuously strive for greater self-awareness. In a sense, to know oneself is a prerequisite for making everything else that we do meaningful and worthwhile. The technical know-how we acquire in science, finance, and computers teaches us how to manipulate nature and sort information, but by itself it tells us nothing about what it means to be a human being. It offers little, if any, insight into our role at this time in the history of the universe, nor does it shed much light on the best way to live our lives. A sound education helps us to gain insight into these questions by inviting us to study and reflect on the thoughts and ideas of those who have devoted their lives to these questions. As E. F. Schumacher explains, in an essay entitled "Education Is Our Greatest Resource," if one never learns the second law of thermodynamics his life will not suffer in any dramatic way. However, if one never reads Shakespeare, or does not get the equivalent of Shakespeare from some other source, the quality of his life suffers immeasurably.[1] For Schumacher, Shakespeare represents a body of wisdom that provides insight into the central issues of human life. Shakespeare portrays the perennial conflicts, temptations, and tragedies with which human beings perpetually wrestle. In doing so, he reveals the psychological, emotional, carnal, and spiritual prototypes of human life. In watching a Shakespeare performance or reading his texts, we can identify with the characters because we struggle with similar issues in our own lives. One of the invaluable benefits of interacting with Shakespeare and other thinkers who uncover the conflicts of the human soul is that we can witness the inevitable fallout that follows the decisions we make and the paths we choose. We can anticipate the fall and the pain that will come to us if we allow ourselves to become enthralled with power, lust, or greed. We can identify critical turning points that determine the fate of a particular character. In doing so, we can foresee the same moments in our own lives with the wisdom of having experienced them vicariously through another. Shakespeare invites us to reflect on our own lives by identifying with the experiences of the characters in his works. Such reflection leads to greater self-awareness, greater wisdom, and a greater life.

If we never reflect upon our own mortality, on love, deceit, power, betrayal, and other issues that determine our fate, we relinquish the input we can and are expected to have on our own lives. We leave the most significant events of our lives to chance, while we are blindly led by the values, expectations, and opinions of what philosopher Søren Kierkegaard calls the "herd." The unreflective individual accepts and follows the dictates of common opinion and responds to the world with the psychological patterns and emotional content that he absorbed before he was old enough to reflect on them. The unreflective person has little to do or say about who he is and who he will become. It is the unreflective person who sustains the cycles of contempt that Alice Miller describes in *The Drama of the Gifted Child*.[2] If we do not uncover the patterns of the unconscious, we are likely to repeat the behavior that we observed and absorbed as children, before we could think and choose for ourselves. The insights of the great thinkers can show us the way out of these cycles, if we appropriate them in a serious and authentic way.

Therefore, education ought to be an arena that encourages and facilitates self-reflection. In studying the classic thinkers of our intellectual tradition we can compare the values and beliefs they articulate with those by which we live. We can ask ourselves what we really think about the issues that define who we are, such as immortality, justice, beauty, compassion, and love. Is there an afterlife? How does my belief about the afterlife impact my daily life? Do I believe that it is better to be just? Or do I agree with the sophist, Thrasymachus, who argues that we want only to appear just. From Thrasymachus' point of view, if we thought we could get away with being unjust, we would, because human beings are interested only in experiencing the base pleasures in life. We obey the law because we are fearful that we might be punished, not because we want to do what is right. Of course, Socrates disagrees. But we need to work through these debates for ourselves to understand what motivates us to act as we do. If I believe that justice is worthwhile for its own sake, what prevents me from being just? To answer such a question and to overcome the obstacles that prevent one from living according to one's ideals is the work of a virtuous and, ultimately, fulfilled soul. Furthermore, a reflective life leads us to examine the uses for which we develop new technologies and ask ourselves if we really need the latest, newest, or flashiest gadget, or if we would be better off living a simpler, less dependent existence. These are the questions that Plato and Aristotle, and Shakespeare, and Tolstoy, and Joyce force us to reckon with. In taking these thinkers and their ideas seriously, we shed light on the issues that define our own lives. We break out of the self-destructive patterns of behavior that we have been developing since infancy. In the process we develop a higher sense of self and live a more meaningful, more fulfilling life. Until we wrestle with these fundamental questions, the amount of money we make and the type of car we drive are mere diversions that distract us from dealing with the crucial issues of human life. All of the trappings of modern-day success will leave us feeling hopelessly empty if we have not worked through the fundamental issues of human existence. Education should alert us to this fact and provide us with the insight and wisdom we need to address these experiences in a healthy and intelligent way. An education that fails to do this is incomplete.

Parents should be interested in their children developing the skills that will enable them to earn a good living. This is a necessary function in modern life. But parents must also understand that their children will have to reflect on life's central issues in order to make good decisions and to lead a fulfilling life. In guiding our children through the educational process, we must take their emotional, psychological, and spiritual development seriously. Hence we should encourage them to reflect on the ideas and thinkers that will provide them with insight into these areas of life. This is not to say that we should discourage their interest in technical fields. As my religion professor said to me when I first told him that I was majoring in economics, "that's good. We need good people in all fields." We need economists who understand the importance of justice. We need doctors who are guided by a sense of compassion. We need administrators who are driven by the pursuit of excellence. We need scientists who understand the significance of their data about the universe. We need stories that can bring new discoveries into the consciousness of nonscientists, so that human beings, as a species, can gain a better understanding of our place in evolutionary history. These stories do not need to be written from scratch. They are already written in the canons of history. Our job as parents and educators is to rewrite and retell them to our children, so that they can incorporate the wisdom of the ages into their own world and their own lives.

How Can Education Work?

Erik Erikson identifies trust as the first essential quality in a healthy personality. With a basic sense of trust toward the world, one can develop other important character traits, such as autonomy and self-reliance. Without trust, it becomes very difficult, if not impossible, to develop a healthy relationship to the world. A lack of trust leads to doubt, suspicion, and anxiety. In an educational setting, trust is a prerequisite for learning. If a student does not trust his teacher, if he is predisposed to thinking that the teacher is trying to mislead him, he will not try to understand what is being taught. Rather, the student will try to identify the deception in what the teacher says. On the other hand, if a teacher does not trust her students, the students will learn to distrust themselves.

This same pattern can be expanded to explain the way that we appropriate knowledge as a culture. We can either offer a preliminary sense of trust to the tradition that is handed down to us, as we try to understand what it is saying, or we can assume that it has nothing to teach us and respond only with criticism and suspicion. Such an outright rejection of tradition may lead to exciting rhetoric about the evil of our predecessors and the untamed freedom of the present. But such rhetoric ultimately rings hollow when it fails to initiate or contribute to more intelligent and healthy ways of life. Just as an individual student must have an initial sense of trust in order to learn what is being taught, we as a culture need to acknowledge that among all the mistakes that have been passed down through centuries of intellectual and cultural history, there is also a great deal of wisdom. I am not suggesting that we should naively accept knowledge on the basis of authority or tradition. But in order to mine the body of wisdom that we have at our disposal, we do need an initial sense of trust. Before we can know where the tradition leads us astray, we must understand the tradition and appropriate its wisdom to benefit our own time. The responsible transmission of knowledge involves critique, but it must begin with trust.

When one does a careful study of the intellectual and cultural traditions that have shaped our current approach to education, it becomes painfully evident that we have been led astray in some fundamental ways. One area in which this is true is the neglect of the body in the learning process. As pointed out above, the structure of many schoolrooms demonstrates a disregard for the body by requiring that children sit still for hours at a time, while information is transmitted almost exclusively through verbal language. The suppression of the body's language, which processes so much of our experience on a preverbal, preconscious level, leads to a disintegration of the learning process. Whereas the seven-year-old German boy learned by integrating different media of communication and knowledge, our students are forced to learn almost exclusively through one medium. Because we have structured education around this one medium, the standards to which we hold our children are pathetically narrow and low. As the spurious cry goes out for higher standards in education, the device used to measure and enforce them is standardized tests. This testing process dramatically confines and compromises the educational experience of students by forcing them to learn and express their knowledge in one way. By learning to submit to this process, students also learn to distrust their own body of knowledge and wisdom, which has been passed on to them through the ancient and unfathomable refinement of their personal and cultural inheritance. Students are trained to disregard visceral responses to their experience. Yet, it is the visceral experience of the world on which the intellectual experience is based. Just as we need a primary sense of trust in order to develop the higher qualities of a healthy personality, the visceral, embodied experience of the world necessarily precedes the intellectual experience. If we did not establish an intimate, preconceptual relationship with the world through touch, smell, taste, and vision, we would have nothing to think about with the intellect.

The basic elements of our personalities are formed early in life, before the intellectual faculties are operative. These basic elements are carved out in neurological and cellular patterns that constitute the evolving expressions of our genetic and cultural inheritance. To eliminate this vast domain of knowledge and wisdom from the educational experience of children is an injustice against their human potential. If those who are crying out for higher educational standards are authentic, they will not measure the accomplishments of students by standardized tests exclusively. They will also measure students' achievements against the potential children bring to the educational experience. This potential requires a diverse and integrated process of learning, in which the material that is being transmitted takes on real significance in the lives of our children.

I found an example of such an integrated process in one of the classrooms I visited at the Early Childhood Center at Sarah Lawrence College. The teacher, Sonna, is gifted at learning the interests and skills of her students and integrating them into the curriculum as the school year progresses. Last year, for instance, after the first month of school, she realized that her students had a strong interest in woodworking. She thought that they could develop that interest into a large group project.[3] During the group discussions that are a regular part of the students' school day, she solicited their ideas as to the type of project they might do. They decided on building a tree house that would become a permanent part of the classroom environment. With the guidance of a class mother who is an artist and a carpenter, the students designed the tree house and traveled to a lumberyard to get the materials. They measured the dimensions of the structure and its constituent pieces, adding and subtracting numbers on the measuring tape. They learned to use tools such as hammers in building the house. They learned new language skills by documenting the work they were doing at different stages of the project. They observed the seasons and how they could affect the appearance of the tree house, and decided to design the steps as fallen leaves in autumn. When the project was complete, Sonna had the children draft a set of rules that would govern the use and care of the tree house. These rules were then posted on the tree house. Not only did the children master the basics of reading, writing, and arithmetic, but they also developed and expressed their own creativity. They not only learned essential academics; they also learned to trust in their own ideas. They learned to respect what *they* felt was interesting and important; because their teacher respected what they thought was important. Unlike many traditional approaches to education, Sonna's did not stifle the enthusiasms of youth by making students conform to a preestablished curriculum. Instead, she identified the spark of their enthusiasm and provided a context in which they could allow that spark to grow into a flame of passionate interest and concern. She trusted in her students, and the students trusted in themselves and in her.

Trust in a teacher and in the information she conveys is necessary at the initial stages of learning. But it is equally essential to teach children to trust in their visceral responses to the world. We need to bring visceral awareness into the educational process by helping students identify the feelings, moods, and emotions that correspond with their actions and behavior. For instance, instead of just asking them for answers to specific questions or problems, we could ask them how it feels to welcome a classmate to school with a handshake or a hug. Or we could ask them how it feels to be excluded or to exclude another from a group. Or, in addition to asking them to solve difficult problems, we could ask them how it feels to solve a difficult problem. Or we could also ask them how it feels not to be prepared for class. When students are made aware of their visceral experience of the world, they learn the limits and boundaries that have been developed and passed on for generations before them. They realize that *their own* rules, personally inscribed in their own flesh, lead to acceptable and productive behavior, not just the rules of teachers and parents. They discover their own interests and talents, not those that others find fashionable. These discoveries are the sparks that can ignite into a lifelong passion for learning.

Let me conclude my remarks on education with a reminder from Aristotle. He writes, "our predecessors render us the double service of hitting off the truth for us or missing the mark and so challenging us to get to the root of the matter ourselves."[4] There are two legacies that our predecessors pass on to us that are instrumental in shaping the educational landscape. The first is our intellectual or cultural legacy, through which bodies of knowledge and wisdom are passed from generation to generation. This legacy must be appropriated with critical care. To reject this tradition outright because of its shortcomings is to pass over generations of refined wisdom. On the other hand, a blind or naive acceptance of this tradition can lead us astray. For instance, in this chapter, we critically appropriated the insights of Plato by drawing on his idea of the soul to point out the danger of overemphasizing appetitive motivations. But we also distanced ourselves from Plato by identifying the body as a source of wisdom and higher educational standards. For Plato, the body is an obstacle to wisdom. I am suggesting that the body's inherited wisdom, which has been comprehensively and systematically dismissed from mainstream education, constitutes the second inherited legacy on which a sound education must be based.

As parents and teachers, we try to hit the mark for our children by rendering intelligible and meaningful the common world we share. But we must recognize that we do not have all of the answers, and we often do miss the mark. So along with doing our best to render the world intelligible, we must give children the confidence and the skills to discover the world for themselves. By allowing children to trust in themselves, in their ideas, feelings, moods, and abilities, we give them an opportunity to discover at least some of the refined wisdom they have inherited through their genetic coding. Our approach to education has suppressed this ancient body of wisdom, at great cost to our children. If parents and teachers could help students to become aware of their own abilities and wisdom by educating the whole child rather than just the intellectual child, we would go a long way toward igniting the passion for learning we all wish our children could carry forth into adulthood. It is invigorating to visit the classrooms of teachers who educate the whole child by developing students' interests, addressing the carnal responses they have to different situations, and making knowledge directly relevant to their lives. To see the immense potential that children of all backgrounds bring to the educational process is almost dizzying. It is heartwarming to see that potential being carried forth under the direction of talented teachers. Unfortunately, for now, these classrooms are the exceptions, and it is clear that there is immense potential going unrealized in too many of our children. Until educational administrators and political leaders recognize this fact and muster the resolve to make revolutionary changes, the trend of parents taking charge of their children's education will continue to grow.

Notes

1. E. F. Schumacher, *Small Is Beautiful: Economics As If People Mattered* (New York: Harper and Row, 1989), 83ff.

2. Alice Miller, *The Drama of the Gifted Child: The Search for the True Self* (New York: Basic Books, 1997).

3. For a detailed account of this project, see Sonna Schupak, *Children as Teachers* (Bronville: Sarah Lawrence College Press, forthcoming).

4. Aristotle, *De Anima*, in *The Basic Works of Aristotle*, ed. Richard McKeon. (New York: Random House, 1968), 538.

PART II

~

PARENTAL VIRTUES

CHAPTER SIX

Courage and Compassion

Although this is the sixth chapter of nine in this book, it is one of the few written after September 11, 2001. As I write, it is a short time after that tragic day, and the fallout is only beginning to be felt. Families and friends are torn apart, and memorial services are being held without the deceased. The wounds are deep, and the healing will be slow. As we struggle to make sense of the events of that day, there are a few things that have been revealed to us already. One thing we can be certain about is that the sense of security that we felt in this country will be difficult to recover. As a result, the anxiety level is rising and will remain higher than it was prior to September 11. For those who have lost family and friends, life will never be the same. But in the midst of overwhelming sadness, we have come to realize the depth of courage and compassion that resides in the souls of human beings.

The images of professional and volunteer rescue workers sifting through rubble, hoping to find human remains, mean different things to different people. My brother is a New York City firefighter who worked long hours at the disaster site. Despite his firsthand knowledge of the site and its sights, I too relied on the news accounts to learn of the courage and heroism of the rescue workers. I did not have any inside information, because, true to his character, my brother did not tell of his acts of heroism. He does not speak about what he does or what he sees. Part of the reason for his silence, I suppose, is that he does not want to relive what he saw more than he has to. But the other part—and this has been his way throughout his life—is that he does not need or seek the praise and honor that come from broadcasting acts of heroism. I am not surprised by what I see in the rescue effort, because I have seen some of those same qualities exemplified by my brother throughout our lives. I have always known what the world is now learning about people like him; at the core of human beings there is a soul of infinite courage and compassion.

Unfortunately, it often takes the worst of situations to bring out the best in human nature. Most of the time, we are so preoccupied with our own interests we fail to draw on our deep and powerful reserves of courage and compassion for others. The days following the terrorist attacks in New York revealed just how far human beings can and will go to help others in need. They will put their own lives in danger to save others. Thousands of volunteers were compelled to offer their services, their blood, and their money to help the victims. Fear and anxiety, the enemies of courage, were nowhere to be found in the eyes or hearts of those rescue workers. Through them we have learned what we are capable of in times of disaster.

As parents we are rarely called to such dramatic acts of courage, and yet courage is perhaps the virtue most called on in good parenting. As parents we face difficult decisions every day regarding the welfare of our children. These decisions, if they are made for the benefit of our children, often require us to resist and overcome formidable obstacles. These obstacles appear in many different forms, ranging from the powerful tide of social expectations and popular culture to medical injuries and disabilities. To make the best decisions in the interest of our children requires courage, conviction, and compassion. If we had any doubt before September 11, we now know that the human organism is endowed with ample reserves of these qualities if we only search for them. As parents seeking to navigate and lead our children through the pitfalls and distractions of the modern world, it is in our interest to tap into these reserves as often and as deeply as possible.

The Courage to Be . . .

In *The Courage to Be*, theologian Paul Tillich describes courage as "self-affirmation in spite of that which tends to prevent the self from affirming itself."[1] For Tillich, the courageous person affirms the most essential parts of the self over the less essential. Such affirmation is no easy task, since there are many parts to the self competing to be expressed. As a result, we often find ourselves experiencing internal conflicts. For instance, on the one hand, I want to go to my favorite restaurant, and on the other, I want to exercise to stay in shape. I want to devote time to spiritual practice, and I want to be entertained. One possibility offers a more immediate pleasure while the other presents pain or sacrifice, hopefully to be followed by a deeper level of satisfaction. Each desire pulls me in a different direction.

To make the best decision in situations of internal conflict, one must prioritize and pursue that which is a higher priority. But to do so means to sacrifice that which is less of a priority. It also means denying that part of the self that desires one activity instead of another. That is, in choosing our highest priorities, we not only affirm a part of the self, we also negate or deny a part of ourselves. Such negation is the primary source of fear and anxiety in human life. Courage is the virtue that overcomes fear and anxiety.

Courage and Fear

Fear and anxiety stem from the same fundamental or ontological source. Both anxiety and fear are experienced as a threat to one's person, one's being, to the fullness of one's existence. Each introduces the possibility of negating or denying possibilities for one's self. Unlike anxiety, fear has an identifiable source that allows for, or invites, or demands our participation. Fear is a privation of anxiety. Whereas anxiety is usually experienced as a background of foggy or vague discomfort, an unidentifiable threat, fear is a concentration of anxiety into a specific source or situation. For parents, fear for our children is encountered often, and it usually demands important and immediate decisions on their behalf.

A Courageous Decision

At the age of seven, I managed to present my parents with an opportunity to make courageous decisions on my behalf. While playing in the hallway of my parent's house, my sister and I engaged in a jocular contest in which she would quickly open and close the front door, baiting me to try getting in. After failing to react quickly enough on the first few attempts, I decided to dive for the door the next time she opened it. Unfortunately, it was a French door with glass panels. I missed the wood frame at the side of the door and put my hand through one of the windowpanes. I remember looking at my hand as it went through and not seeing any blood. But I panicked and pulled it back as fast as I could, slicing it along the broken shards that remained in the door.

I could tell by the reaction of the adults at the hospital that my condition wasn't good. After they had controlled the bleeding in the emergency room, I was assigned to a room in the hospital, where I received many visitors and many more cans of Seven-Up and cookies. I didn't understand much of the conversations that these visitors were having with my parents, but I knew that there was serious concern. I remained in a bed for almost a week, during which I received only cursory medical treatment, while we waited for a surgeon to look at my hand.

My father, a quiet and reserved man, listened to the explanations of the staff each day, almost always transmitted through my mother. Finally, after days without any treatment or useful information, he told them he was taking me home. I remember my mother crying in the hospital room, worried that he was making a mistake. The hospital sent their important people to tell my father that the only way he could take me home was to sign waivers saying that he was taking me against doctor's orders. He asked for the papers and I was home that evening.

I recall that it was nice to be home. But there was work to be done. My mother was on the phone to everyone she knew in the medical field. One of her friends was a nurse at Montefiore Hospital. She recommended a hand surgeon named Dr. Lewin. I went to see him the next day, and I was in surgery a couple of days later. Dr. Lewin and his staff saved my right hand. If my father had not had the courage to go against the "experts" at the first hospital, I would have had a very different life.

Parents are constantly faced with decisions that will indelibly impact the lives of their children. In my case, it would have been understandable for my father to follow the advice of the first hospital. Thankfully he did not. Like so many parents, my father was not willing to accept mediocrity when it came to the health, education, or well-being of his children. But parents face great obstacles in achieving the goals they have for themselves as providers for their children. They often find themselves competing against a culture of mediocrity when it comes to caring for their children and instilling in them the values they need to succeed in finding fulfillment in their lives. With the ever-present message of advertisers telling children that happiness is to be found in their next purchase, parents are constantly challenged to convince their children (and themselves) that there is something more to life than being the most powerful consumer.

This is a difficult challenge, not just because of the enormous number of things and messages vying for the attention of children, but also because parents must resist the temptation to adopt the social values that target them. Parents are called to be courageously steadfast in living and sharing their own values and wisdom if they are to demonstrate the importance of overcoming the empty mind-set of consumerism and immediate gratification.

In making decisions for their children, parents must often overcome fear: fear of the situation or fear of making the wrong decision. As with any parent who sees his child injured, I am sure that my father feared that my hand would not heal properly regardless of what he or the doctors did. But the situation called for a response. The source of his fear was clearly defined. This fear called on his deep reserves of courage to overcome the problem in the best possible way. On making the decision to seek better care, he must also have had to face the fear that his decision could have been the wrong one. But a courageous person accepts the possibility and the responsibility that his decision may lead to the wrong or less desired result.

The courageous person who has the insight to know what is to be done understands that in choosing one possibility we forgo other possibilities. This is a part of the human condition. It is what Heidegger refers to as *being-guilty*.[2] Heidegger is not referring to the moral sense of guilt that occurs when one feels bad about having done something wrong or immoral. He means that there are only so many possibilities that we can choose. Once we choose one possibility, there are others that are lost. The inability to choose each and every possibility that presents itself to us can leave us with a feeling of emptiness or a lack, a sense of incompleteness. It is this sense of incompleteness that Heidegger identifies as guilt.

The advantage of experiencing fear rather than anxiety is that fear usually makes the choices we have very clear. It defines a situation and the possibilities we can choose. In my father's case, the fear was that I would loose the use of my right hand. The choice my father was faced with was either to leave me where I was and trust the word of a staff that seemed unreliable to him, or to make the courageous move by going against the experts and seeking better care. This was not an easy choice to make, but his courage enabled him to make the right one.

Following Tillich's formulation, my father's decision was courageous because it affirmed the more essential parts of himself over and against the less essential. In this case, it was less essential that he be cooperative and deferential, even though he knew less about the medical details than those with whom he was disagreeing. While he has the ability to be cooperative and deferential, and it is sometimes necessary to be so, he did not allow these qualities to interfere with his understanding of what needed to be done. Instead, he affirmed and honored qualities that were more essential in this situation, namely his intuition for sensing reliability and competence.

He was also affirming his authority as a concerned parent. While it would have been understandable for him to defer to the hospital staff, to do so would have gone against his character, which told him to do everything he could, with the limited knowledge available to him, to make things right. He was unwilling to relinquish his parental authority and role as primary caregiver until he was satisfied with those to whom he was transferring it. In this case the stakes were high and very immediate. He had to decide quickly, and the consequences of his decision would be known almost immediately.

While most parents do not have to make such dramatic decisions very often, they do make important decisions daily. These decisions range from which television program children should watch or what food they should eat to what school they should go to or whether or not they should drive to a party where it is likely that alcohol will be used. In all of these decisions, parents are challenged to affirm and express the more essential parts of the self over the less essential. This is courage. But in order to have courage, to make courageous decisions, to affirm what they value the most, parents must first be clear about what it is they value and the behavior they want to exemplify for their children. In a world that is so full of mixed messages and questionable ideals, this is no easy task. It requires serious self-examination. It demands that parents reflect on the habits of behavior that they express on a daily basis and the ideals that they hold to be true and good. Ideally, such reflection allows ours habits to be informed more fully by our ideals.

Courage and Anxiety

While fear is not an emotion or feeling with which one wants to spend much time, it is often much easier to confront than its ontological cousin, anxiety. Fear can be identified. Therefore it can be addressed and responded to with courage. Anxiety is more difficult to identify and therefore more difficult to address. In *The Death of Ivan Ilych*, Leo Tolstoy offers a haunting tale of a life consumed by anxiety and of numerous unsuccessful attempts to overcome it. I find the story haunting because Ivan's life is not very different from those of many people who are considered successful by the standards of contemporary culture. But like so many people chasing a narrow definition of success today, Ivan lacks the ability or the will to engage in serious self-reflection. As a result, he lives an uninspiring life that becomes consumed with despair as he approaches his death. As Tolstoy describes it, his life is "most simple and most ordinary and therefore most terrible."

On the surface, Ivan's life is a success. He has a respectable career as a lawyer and then a judge. He marries a respectable wife and has children with her. They own a house that allows them to imitate the upper class. But all of this cannot help Ivan escape his terrible fate, brought on by a terminal illness. This is the fate of anxiety and despair in the face of death.

Ivan's despair begins to set in as his illness progresses without a diagnosis from the celebrated medical professionals who examine him. With no clear diagnosis, medical protocols are ineffective. Ivan begins to recognize that his doctors are at a loss to understand and treat his condition. What bothers Ivan more than the ineffectiveness of his physicians, however, is the air of authority they try to convey as they lean over his bed without knowing what is ailing Ivan. In trying to preserve their air of authority, the physicians are unwilling to give Ivan a straight answer to his most pressing question: "Will I recover from this ailment?" The physicians, along with Ivan's family, are unwilling to admit that Ivan is dying. Their deception drives Ivan mad.

As Ivan moves closer to death, he finds it almost impossible to find any comfort. The only relief he finds is when the household servant, Gerasim, cares for him by lifting his legs or just sitting with him. He appreciates Gerasim's presence because Gerasim is authentic. He does not try to hide the fact that Ivan is dying. He does what he can to help him. The simplicity and authenticity of Gerasim causes Ivan to reflect on his life. As Ivan looks back on his life to recall happy times, he is repeatedly brought back to childhood. He cannot find any happy memories from his adult life, despite the "propriety" and "success" of it all.

As these realizations come to Ivan, his suffering is magnified. His diseased body begins closing in on him and his pain sears him, along with the increasing awareness that he has not lived as he should have. His physical pain is transforming into a spiritual pain. He cannot understand why someone who lived such a "proper" life should have to experience such suffering. He wallows in self-pity and grows angry with everyone, including God. He wants to blame someone other than himself for his inauthentic life. But there is nobody else to blame, and he has to accept responsibility for the life he has chosen to live. The anxiety that he has subdued throughout his life by losing himself in pleasantries and casual distractions can no longer be hidden. It reaches a fever pitch just before his death, and he screams in agony for days.

But as long as he is alive, Ivan thinks, even if he has not lived as he should have, there is still a chance to make things right. At the very end of his life, as he is dying, his son comes to visit him. As Ivan's body is flailing in pain, his hand touches his son. Ivan looks up to see his son crying. For the first time, Ivan transcends his narcissistic self-absorption to feel pity for someone else. He finally realizes that he is not the only person to suffer, and he begins to feel compassion for others, even for his wife. With his last breath he tries to ask for his wife's forgiveness. He has only enough strength to say, "forgo." With his transformation from a self-absorbed, self-pitying individual to a compassionate, understanding, and contrite self, Ivan no longer fears death and no longer feels the pain of his disease. By finding compassion and concern for others, he also finds the courage to face death and overcome the despair of realizing he has lived an inauthentic life.

Ivan's journey toward death is a good example of what Martin Heidegger describes as *Being-toward-death*.[3] For Heidegger, there are two ways one can approach death, inauthentic and authentic. For most of his life, Ivan is inauthentic. He uses his activities, including his career, as diversions. He appeals to his superiors to approve of his life without taking the time to figure out the best way to live on his own. He is caught up in the opinion of the many, rather than discovering how to be true to himself.

An essential part of being authentic or true to oneself is to face up to one's own reality and one's own death. Authenticity demands that we consciously and courageously acknowledge our mortality. In doing so, we experience the call of conscience. This call pulls us out of the diversions of everyday life and the idle chatter of constant company to be alone in silence. The call of conscience does not provide specific instructions about how to live. It merely provides us with space in which we can prioritize our lives. That is, by taking one's own reality and one's death seriously, one can begin to understand what is most important about life and find the courage to choose those possibilities, rather than blindly follow the opinions of the many. For Ivan, it takes a terminal illness and reflections on his deathbed for him to courageously choose his greatest possibility, namely, compassion for his family.

Tolstoy's account of existence in the face of imminent death and the despair it can cause serves as a chilling reminder to take our lives seriously. Nobody wants to look back on his or her life to feel only regret and despair. While it seems that our culture promotes the pursuit of superficial or inauthentic lives, and that many lack the courage to resist these temptations, there are unique individuals who do resist. Some of these courageous people are parents who overcome anxiety-ridden lives without going through the darkness of existential despair. I think of parents who are faced with the enormous task of raising children with mental and physical disabilities. Beyond the initial shock of learning that an infant is disabled and will remain so, parents who courageously choose to devote their lives to caring for their disabled children must confront the anxiety of raising a child who is different, not only from other children, but from what is so familiar to the parents. In *Love's Labor*, for instance, Eva Kittay describes the difficulty of coming to terms with the fact that the life of the mind, of reflection and clear, rational thinking, which was so central to who she was, would not be possible for her daughter. Imagine the anxiety of charting a future, of finding goals for a child who will never do the most basic things her parents do. Kittay was open-minded and courageous enough to discover, to learn, that what she had thought was most important about human life really was not. She learned from her daughter, who would never think or speak in the ways that Kittay valued so much, that love was more central, more fundamental to human life, to being a human being, than reason. While Kittay's moving description of her relationship with her daughter does not mention the virtue of courage, she and her husband have shown heroic portions of courage on a daily basis for more than twenty years. They never gave in to pressure to abandon their daughter, even though caring for her would dramatically change their lives. They are models of compassion and courage.

I also think of our friends Eddie and Antoinette O'Grady, who discovered that their five-month-old daughter had cancer. Her prognosis indicated a less than 20-percent survival rate. As a result of the best medical care possible and superhuman parental devotion, their child is thriving, though they still live with the anxiety of residual heart ailments and regular tests to detect possible relapses. In order to meet the developmental needs of their daughter, who is now five, and allow her to experience the comforts and joys of childhood, they must constantly overcome the daily anxiety their daughter's health provokes. This takes courage. Like Eva Kittay, they affirm the most essential parts of their lives in the face of the persistent threat of despair. They have the courage to embrace life, their own and their daughter's, without wallowing in how it could have been. Rather than seeking pity from others, they attend conferences to assist other families facing the same battles. This takes compassion and courage. They have the courage to act on what is most central to who they are, namely, love and compassion. They may not have known this before their child's illness, but they have clearly prioritized their values and their lives in response to her illness. Less courageous parents may not be capable of allowing love and compassion to prevail over despair.

Finally, I think of Roger Gottlieb's analysis of his role as father of his fifteen-year-old daughter Esther. In *Joining Hands: Politics and Religion Together for Social Change*, Gottlieb demonstrates the extraordinary effort that goes into parenting a child with multiple disabilities and impairments. Like Kittay, Gottlieb reveals the social and political failures in the prevailing attitudes toward and treatment of people with disabilities. But what I find most impressive is his courage to face up to the reality of his and his daughter's situation. This reality not only involves uncountable medical visits and enormous out-of-pocket expenses; it also involves protecting his daughter from the cruelty of people who will shun or ridicule her. It involves accepting the fact that she will never go to summer camp or college. It means that every daily and weekly schedule he makes must account for him or his wife being around the house for their daughter. It even includes the anxiety of thinking about Esther's future when her parents are no longer around to care for her. In spite of these anxiety-provoking difficulties, Gottlieb has the courage to face up to his reality honestly and see his role as a parent as a spiritual test, an opportunity for growth through self-sacrifice, compassion, and love. He writes,

> In my case, parenting dilemmas are a ceaseless reminder that despite my persistent efforts, what I can accomplish is really very limited. Esther is, in this sense, a persistent sign that while I should do my best to teach and help her, that the most important thing I can offer her is simply a kind of love and acceptance which she may not get elsewhere and which in any case she really needs from her father. For me this is a spiritual test of the highest order, for it requires that I overcome my narcissistic interpretation of her fate. Who, after all, told me that I was God and had the power to heal what is broken in the world?[4]

Gottlieb is realistic, and his realism leads to a spiritual life grounded in love and compassion.

These parents are special. They exemplify a distinctive character in response to difficult circumstances. They are special because they have the courage to face reality, no matter how difficult, rather than run from it. They embrace the difficulties life has dealt them and respond with love, courage, and compassion.

Along with Tolstoy's stark reminder of the difference between an inauthentic and an authentic life, these parents reveal the importance of courage and compassion as virtues for becoming good parents. By facing up to our own situations and to our own deaths, we are forced to prioritize our choices in life. We become acutely aware that there are a limited number of possibilities that we can actually pursue and a limited amount of time to accomplish those things that are most important to us. Facing up to one's reality and one's mortality is the most powerful way to develop an authentic and fulfilling life. It helps us to strip away what is nonessential to who we are and want to be and to identify the paths of enthusiasm that are so abundant in childhood, but often forgotten under the pressures of adulthood. As the O'Gradys, Roger Gottlieb, and Eva Kittay demonstrate, the most bountiful enthusiasms of life are found in caring for their children even under the most difficult circumstances.

Courage, Compassion, and Joy

But we need not rely only on the examples of adults in our search for models of courage and compassion. Those of us who find ourselves losing some of the enthusiasms of youth might learn something from children, who still live with and act on their enthusiasms. These enthusiasms are often free expressions of virtue: expressions of compassion and courage, which often get smothered under the busyness and self-interest of adult life. These virtues drive special parents like the O'Gradys, Gottlieb, and Kittay. These virtues were uncovered in the acts of rescue workers after September 11. The intensity of these situations allows the primal instincts for care and compassion to emerge from beneath the shattered sense of self and society. While the whole world has seen a dramatic example of these primal instincts at work, they are often on display in more subtle ways in the daily lives of children.

A Friendly Rescue

My four-year-old, Caitriona, and her eleven-year-old cousin, Brighid, attend swimming lessons in the same program, but on different levels. An uncompromising director runs the program with discipline and precision. The rules are made known with no uncertainty to both the swimmers and to the parents. But the results she produces are superior, and few, if any, question the methods or tone of her leadership.

Most children who join the program can swim before they join. Caitriona could not. She was learning for the first time, and she began the program a couple of weeks late. As the twelve-week program drew to a close, she was behind the others in her group. Her teacher was very patient and very effective. She made the lessons fun and gave Caitriona the attention she needed to make up most of the ground she had lost by starting late.

On the last night of their twelve-week program, Caitriona and Brighid traveled together to their lessons. Brighid's lesson was the hour after Caitriona's, so she changed into her swimsuit to watch Caitriona's lesson. On this night, Caitriona's teacher was called away from the pool at the start of the lesson. To keep things moving, the director filled in, getting the young children started. She didn't know that Caitriona was behind the others. As she does with her own classes, she gave instructions to the group as a whole. She wanted them to swim to the other end of the pool using one kind of stroke and swim back using another. She demonstrated the strokes for each swimmer as he or she began. Caitriona looked bewildered by the directness of the instructions, but when her turn came she did her part. She jumped in and began to swim toward the other end of the pool. She had never swum that distance before.

As Caitriona began her epic journey, her instructor returned and saw Brighid standing at the end of the pool. She told Brighid to walk alongside the pool to give Caitriona encouragement. Just before the halfway point,

Caitriona looked up and caught Brighid's eye. The look on Caitriona's face was one of uncertainty on the verge of panic. Brighid understood what Caitriona's face was saying and instinctively she dove into the pool, swimming under Caitriona, and coming up on the other side of her. Brighid swam next to her until they reached the end of the pool. The parents watching were amazed by Brighid's action, in part because nobody was sure what the director would say, since Brighid had blatantly broken the rules, but mostly because of the maturity of her concern and her decisiveness to act. When the girls reached the end, the director joined the other parents in cheering for both Brighid and Caitriona. Thrilled with having swum the length of the pool for the first time, Caitriona jumped back in and swam to the other end on her own.

Brighid was acting on the same primal instincts of compassion and courage that have been cultivated by the special parents who care for their children under the most difficult circumstances and the rescue workers who risk their lives to save others. While children can be mean to each other from time to time, they are more likely than adults to exemplify the primal virtues of courage and compassion on a regular basis. One reason that children are more likely to act on these instincts is that they have yet to develop the clinging needs of the adult ego. Because they are still guided by the enthusiasms of youth and have yet to develop the constraints of egoistic need, which can smother virtuous instincts residing deep within the human soul, children often act on these virtues instinctively. These virtues are closer to the surface of their personalities. In contrast, adults who have lost the enthusiasms of life try to compensate for their loss by feeding the needs generated by the ego. These needs and the activities required to procure them often lead us down paths of self-alienation. That is, we forget or lose touch with those activities that allow the energy of life to pulsate through our flesh and animate our bones.

As parents, we want to be courageous for and compassionate toward our children. We want to express the essential parts of the self over and against the less essential parts of the self. In doing so we can uncover these primal virtues and serve as strong beacons to guide the paths of our children. However, these primal virtues are hidden and unavailable to us as long as we fail to overcome the fear and anxiety that accompanies unreflective or inauthentic adulthood. Overcoming fear and anxiety demands that we find the enthusiasms of life by carefully choosing our priorities and living them out. We can take the life of Ivan Ilych as a warning of what lies ahead for those of us who fail to reflect on the fundamental questions of life. We can look to the courageous examples of special parents like the O'Gradys, Roger Gottlieb, and Eva Kittay, as well as to children, for examples of primal, uninhibited courage and compassion. The reserves of such virtue are available to us all. But we must do the preliminary work of discarding the superficial and distracting needs of the self-interested ego to tap into these reserves. When we do, we will have the resources we need to make wise decisions for our children as well as the conviction to stand by them.

Notes

1. Paul Tillich, *The Courage to Be* (New Haven, Conn.: Yale University Press, 1952), 32.

2. Martin Heidegger, *Being and Time*, trans. John Macquarrie and Edward Robinson (New York: Harper and Row, 1962), 325–27.

3. Heidegger, *Being and Time*, 279ff.

4. Roger Gottleib, *Joining Hands: Politics and Religion Together for Social Change* (Boulder: Westview, 2002).

CHAPTER SEVEN

Integrity

For the past few years, *The Sopranos* has been one of the most popular programs on television. The show portrays the lives of members of organized crime in northern New Jersey and their families. The characters enjoy the material luxury that accompanies organized crime, but their lives are corrupted by deceit, violence, and murder. Tony Soprano is the boss of the organization. He commands a group of loyal, but sociopathic "soldiers" who often use violence to enforce his will. Tony is also a husband and the father of two children: Anthony, his teenage son, and Meadow, a first-year college student. Tony tries to live a double life by keeping his criminal activities, which include extortion and murder, and his social life, highlighted by mistresses and strip clubs, separate and hidden from his family.

The show responsibly reveals that such a separation is not possible. Although Tony has achieved the financial means to provide his family with a large house and many expensive amenities, his life of crime also has unsavory consequences. For instance, Tony suffers from intense anxiety attacks, which he tries to overcome by undergoing psychotherapy. Even in psychotherapy, however, Tony is unwilling to open himself to the source of his problems. He brushes past his relationship with his mother and refuses to discuss his life of crime. As a result, he fails to make significant progress in therapy, though he seems to enjoy the time spent with the therapist.

In addition to anxiety attacks, Tony seems to be losing control of his family life. As his children grow through their teenage years and gain their own perspective on the world, they begin to feel and recognize the tension that their father's lifestyle has inflicted on them. Anthony begins to act out by cheating on exams, destroying school property, and smoking marijuana. He ends up getting expelled from his high school. Frustrated that his son is not living a virtuous and productive life, Tony decides to send him to a military academy. He wants his son to learn discipline. On the day Anthony is leaving for the military academy, he collapses with an anxiety attack.

Tony's daughter, a bright college freshman, begins to experience an acute conflict between loyalty and rebellion in her relationship with her father. She begins to recognize more clearly and despise the deceitful circumstances into which she was born. From the distance of her college dormitory, she sees the tragic and shameful life of her father and his friends. She begins to have a sense of the extent of their crimes and she becomes increasingly disdainful and indignant toward her father and his way of life. Meadow's disgust is clearly revealed in the final episode of the 2001 season, during which Ralph, one of Tony's captains, orders that her former boyfriend, Jackie, be killed.

Jackie was a disinterested college student who found the life of organized crime too alluring to resist. He failed out of school and began working for Ralph, his mother's boyfriend and a captain in the crime family. Seeking to make their mark in organized crime, Jackie, along with a few other young gangsters, decided to rob a card game involving some "made" members of the crime family. Christopher, Tony's nephew and a captain in the family, recognized Jackie under his mask. When the dust settled, one of Jackie's crew was killed after missing the getaway car, and Christopher asked Tony for permission to kill Jackie. Tony refused. He left the decision about what should be done to Jackie to Ralph, the captain under whose jurisdiction the card game had taken place. An unscrupulous and vicious character, Ralph ordered that Jackie be murdered, even though he lived with the boy's mother. Following the murder, he circulated a story that Jackie had been involved with drugs, and this had led to his death.

Meadow did not believe the story about her former boyfriend. She suspected that his murder had something to do with her father's organization. At the reception following Jackie's burial, with alcohol-fueled bravery, she could no longer contain the indignation she felt toward those who were mourning Jackie's death. As Tony's uncle sang a song that moved most of the adults in the room to tears, Meadow began firing tiny balls of bread at people sitting around the room. In the midst of intense sorrow, Meadow saw a roomful of deceitful and callous criminals. She refused to participate in the charade of mourning a death for which they were responsible. She joked while the others cried.

Her father could hardly believe that his daughter was joking at such a serious moment. With a look of disbelief and intense anger, he walked swiftly toward her. Meadow saw him coming and ran out of the building. Her father followed her out screaming at her. She continued running across a busy street with complete disregard for her safety. She was so hurt and disgusted by her family life, it seemed that at that moment she was willing to die just to get away.

While most parents are not involved in criminal activity, this story reveals a deep and tragic irony from which all parents can learn a serious lesson. Children look to their parents for guidance. Even though children go through inevitable periods of resistance, they idolize their parents. Parents are their first and most significant heroes.

Yet we all have flaws. As children mature, they recognize flaws in the character of their parents. As a result, they must adjust their opinion of their parents. If parents are honest with their children and have a healthy, communicative relationship with them, children can adapt to their maturing understanding of their parents without much difficulty. However, if a child learns that the parents are hiding something or that they are engaged in activities that are embarrassing to the child's sense of decency and integrity, it is much more difficult for the child to adjust. The inevitable periods of resistance become extended, often crippling, periods of resentment.

When a child's primary feeling toward a parent is resentment, the expectations, direction, and even support of parents is often interpreted and experienced as an invasion or manipulation. Resentful children do not respond to the demands, aspirations, or expectations of parents who fail to live a life of integrity. Children feel the conflicts and contradictions that parents bring to the dynamics of family life. They quickly recognize when there is a dissonance between what parents demand and expect of them and the values by which their parents live. On recognizing that their parents do not really believe what they tell their children, the children often feel lost and resentful. They feel as though their parents deceived them, and the pain that this causes children often leads to errant and self-destructive behavior. This dynamic is demonstrated by Tony Soprano's children, who carry the intense anguish of children who have been thrown into a family life that is based on deceit. They no longer want to respond to a father who fails to live according to the virtues he expects of them.

So there is a powerful and telling irony to the Soprano story. Tony's sociopathic "soldiers" respond to his demands. To them, Tony is authentic. He does not hold them to a double standard. He lives according to the values by which he expects them to live: deceit, violence, and a disregard for human life. His children, on the other hand, are no longer willing to submit to their father's will, because they sense and see his inauthenticity. They see him as a weak and deceptive character who fails to provide the leadership they need and want as his children. He can control a cast of ruthless murderers, but his children are unresponsive. He lacks integrity and his children lack respect for him.

The Sopranos is a fictional story and it makes clear the lack of integrity that infests Tony's family life and the effects this has on his children. Most parents and most families do not lack integrity to such a degree. Instead, we face a wide variety of smaller issues that test our integrity on a daily basis. For instance, one of my students appealed to me for some philosophical guidance regarding a situation in which her five-year-old daughter was the target of her classmates. Each day she packed lunch for her daughter. Her lunch always included a treat. One day the girl decided to share her treat with one of her friends. As word spread about her generosity, a group of students saw her as a weak target and began to take her lunch.

The mother's eyes filled with tears as she told the story and thought of others taking advantage of her daughter. Along with the other students who were listening, I felt her sorrow. On the one hand, she was trying to raise her daughter to be kind and virtuous. On the other hand, she did not want her daughter to be a reticent victim. She had taken practical steps to address the situation by contacting the school authorities and her daughter's teacher. But she wanted to do more. She wanted the behavior to stop. She wanted her daughter to do her part to stop it, but did not want to encourage her to engage in behavior that would compromise her integrity. She appealed to me as her philosophy teacher for insight as to how she should handle the situation.

I immediately thought of Plato's dialogue "Crito" and the controversial example of parenting that Socrates portrays. But before offering a philosophical perspective on the situation, I wanted to address a couple of points that I thought my student needed to keep foremost in her mind. First, I wanted to reassure her that she should trust her motherly instincts and wisdom to protect her daughter. The pain that she felt for her daughter was a good indication that there was a problem that needed adult intervention. Second, I thought that she should let her daughter know how she felt—she was proud of her daughter for sharing with her friend, but the behavior of the others was unacceptable. Finally, I wanted to encourage her to do what was necessary and appropriate to put an end to other students violating her daughter's property and space.

From what I could discern, the daughter was not interested in fighting back in any overt way. This led me to consider one other point that I could not raise in class. I was hoping that the young girl was not suffering from low self-esteem, which could lead her to think that, somehow, her victim status was deserved. The mother was a very bright, soft-spoken, and loving person. There was no reason to suspect that she was making her daughter feel anything but loved. On the other hand, she was from a very traditional family in India. She was a wife and mother in an arranged marriage. It was possible, I thought, that the child was learning her role as a female in their family structure, which role, unfortunately, is one of subservience. But I could only speculate that this was a possibility, since I did not have an opportunity to explore the situation in detail. What I could share with the mother to give her some philosophical perspective on the situation was a classic story in which parental integrity is portrayed as an essential companion to parental love. The example I had in mind is found in Plato's dialogue entitled "Crito."

Socrates' Parental Legacy

The "Crito," named after Socrates' close friend and interlocutor in the dialogue, reveals the character and thought processes of Socrates two days before he was put to death by the Athenian authorities. Although the charges against Socrates were false, he was convicted and sentenced to death by the court. Among Socrates' close friends was a wealthy man named Crito. He recognized the injustice that was being perpetrated against Socrates and he wanted to help. He came to visit Socrates in his prison cell two days before his execution with a plan for Socrates to escape. He had made arrangements with the security guards and with others on the outside to secure Socrates' safety. He insisted that Socrates leave the prison with him under the cloak of darkness.

To most human beings, this would be an irresistible offer. What could be wrong with preserving one's life in the face of an unjust execution? But Socrates was not like most human beings. He was never impressed with the opinion of the many. He was only interested in what is true and what is right. His tool for determining what is right was reason. So the dialogue with his friend Crito gets under way with an agreement that Socrates will only do what is right as determined by reason. The fact that his life is at stake does not change the principles by which he has always lived.

Crito begins by offering arguments to convince Socrates to escape. The most forceful argument challenges Socrates as a father. Crito argues that Socrates has a responsibility as a father to raise and educate his children. He tells Socrates that by accepting his death he is deserting his own children. He reminds Socrates: "If they do not meet with the usual fate of orphans there will be small thanks to you. Either a man should not beget children, or else he should persevere to the end in their nurture and education. But you appear to be choosing the easier part, not the better and manlier—and all your life you have professed that you cared for virtue."[1]

These are strong words with which most parents might agree. From Crito's point of view, the virtuous thing to do is to escape so that Socrates can continue to be a father to his children.

Socrates does not directly respond to Crito's argument. Instead he convinces Crito that the only question that matters is whether or not, according to the dictates of sound reason, it is right or wrong to escape from prison. Socrates dismisses the charge that he is reneging on his responsibility as a father as an ungrounded opinion of the many. His position is that if he can identify his responsibility as a person, and carry out that responsibility, he will also be meeting his parental responsibilities. To identify his primary responsibility, they would have to explore the issue, as they had done numerous times in the past, through rational dialogue.

Socrates explains that if he escapes from prison, he breaks the laws of Athens, which he has agreed to all his life. In fact, Socrates sees the laws of Athens as parents. Under these laws he was raised and educated. He fought in wars to defend these laws. Since Athens is a democracy, he could have pursued any disagreements with the laws through legal channels. He never did because he agreed with the laws. To break them now, just because they are not working in his favor, would be unjust in his eyes. Such an act would undermine the principle on which he has built his life—never choose wrong over right. To break the law, he must violate his life's principle. And for what? To live a life in exile, running from the law of his home city, which he loves like a parent.

Unlike most people, Socrates does not believe that life should be preserved at all costs. For him, the most important thing is not just living or preserving life. It is a matter of living well. If one upholds the principle of always choosing right instead of wrong, which for Socrates is the guiding principle of the philosophical life, death is nothing to be feared. In living according to this principle, the philosopher is prepared for death. When it comes, he does not try to hide. As Plato explains in the "Apology," "you are wrong if you think a man with a spark of decency ought to calculate life or death; the only thing he ought to consider, if he does anything, is whether he does right or wrong, whether it is what a good man does or a bad man."[2]

By focusing the discussion on the immediate issue at hand, which is whether or not he should escape, Socrates makes the question of right or wrong very clear. Even though the charges against him are false, the laws that his accusers are enforcing are the ones Socrates has always agreed to and upheld. To break them would be wrong. Therefore, Crito's argument concerning his parental responsibility is irrelevant, in the eyes of Socrates. That is not to say that Socrates' children are irrelevant to him. Socrates does not say much about his feelings for his children, so we must interpret his actions in light of the principles by which he lived his life.

If Socrates escapes and undermines his own principles, not only will his accusers gain a great victory by exposing him (and the philosophical life in general) as a fraud; his children will learn a lesson that Socrates is unwilling to teach them. In upholding his principles to his death, Socrates is giving his children a powerful lesson in how they should live their own lives. His uncompromising integrity is something for which they can have the highest respect, and it is a model according to which they can live. After love, or, more accurately, with love, integrity is the one virtue that children want most from their parents. I say *with* love because love without integrity or integrity without love can be confusing and hurtful to children. So in accepting his death because it is the right thing to do, Socrates does not abandon his parental responsibilities. In fact, he upholds them in a way that most of us can only approximate. He teaches his children that it is unacceptable to live a life of compromise, because when one lives a life of virtue, those who lack virtue can never harm one. Even though they can put a man to death they cannot touch his soul.

After I shared the story of Socrates with my student, we agreed that it is extremely difficult to live a life of uncompromising integrity. There are endless obstacles and temptations along the way. Perhaps only the most advanced souls of humanity—such as Socrates, Jesus, the Buddha, Saint Francis, Gandhi, Mother Theresa—can achieve this kind of life. When they do, it often leads to their death, as it did for Socrates. Yet, if we follow the reasoning of Socrates, the alternative to such a life is tragic. For as Socrates famously declares, "the unexamined life is not worth living." The unexamined life, a life of compromise, neglects and corrupts the soul. It forces us to cling to life at all costs and to fear death. It compels us to seek out diversions because we are afraid to examine the state of our souls. It leads to bad decisions, because the things that are most important to achieving a good life fall out of focus. It causes us, as parents, to send conflicting and confusing messages to our children, making us poor leaders and teachers.

On hearing of Socrates' strength and integrity, my student felt much better about the roles into which she and her daughter had been cast as a result of her daughter's generosity. She realized that being in the minority in choosing the path of virtue is difficult, but inevitable. She understood that her daughter was correct and the others were wrong. Although her daughter was suffering pain at the hands of her classmates, the only way they could harm her soul was if they forced her to act as they were acting. Her mother needed the strength to stand by her daughter, to remind her that her virtue is unique and special, and that it is difficult to be uncompromisingly good. Even with the difficulty, to be uncompromisingly good is infinitely better than the alternative.

Disconnected or Detached?

After presenting this account of Socrates and his relationship to his children, another student in the class raised her hand and questioned Socrates' integrity. She pointed out that the conviction with which Socrates chose to accept death rather than live and raise his children might only have been possible for a person who was disconnected from his emotional life. In Socrates, reason seemed to leave no room for emotions, and she questioned the idea that love could be separated from emotions. This was an excellent point, so we explored the role of emotions in parental love. Socrates didn't display his emotions, if he had any. But the question we needed to address was what the absence of an emotional display tells us about Socrates and his relationship to his children.

To understand the role of emotions in parental love, we need to make a distinction between one who is disconnected from emotional life and one who is detached from emotional life. A person becomes disconnected from emotional life when he is unable to appropriate his emotions in a healthy way. Such a person usually represses his emotional life because the experiences of early childhood and adolescence did not allow for these emotions to be expressed and sorted out. As a result, emotions become repressed and jumbled, making them difficult to retrieve and express in the appropriate ways later in life. The disconnection from emotional life that adults carry with them is often very confusing and painful. It clouds the decision-making process and often interferes with the development and expression of self.

When this is the experience of parents, their confusion and anxiety are visited directly on the children. Indecisiveness and a failure to understand the motivations for decisions and actions throw the development of the children and the family into disarray. The leadership and guidance of parents who suffer from a disconnect between the rational and emotional (including psychological and spiritual) life is unpredictable and inconsistent. The lack of healthy emotional integration introduces disruptive detours into the path of a child's self-development.

To be disconnected from emotional life is not the same as having no emotions. In recent times we have seen tragic examples of parents who have failed to effectively integrate their emotional life into a healthy personality. Emotions build power and fury when left unattended. The danger for people who are disconnected from their emotions is that they have little or no control over behavior that emotions can generate. When they encounter situations that call their repressed and misunderstood emotions forth from the unconscious into the light of day, they often become consumed by the emotions. The actions that follow are often regrettable. We have seen the tragic results of parents who lose control of themselves as a result of a perceived injustice against their children. A Massachusetts father beat his son's hockey coach to death in the presence of his children. Parents in Atlanta went to court over the eligibility of a child on a T-ball team and vowed to carry the dispute forward to the following year, when the children would play their first year of little league baseball. (This story was aired as a part of a documentary. While the parents argued, the children interviewed did not even know who had won or lost the game they had just played, as they shared ice cream with their opponents at a picnic table.) A mother's emotional anguish led her to systematically drown her children in the bathtub. As these instances reveal, the love parents have for their children can be easily confused or distorted by a poorly developed or traumatized emotional life. The parental integrity that children long for is elusive for those who have not incorporated their emotional life into their habits of behavior.

I do not believe that a lack of emotional cultivation plagued the relationship Socrates had with his children. As a highly developed individual who spent most of his life nurturing the inner life of his soul, Socrates was acutely aware of the power of emotions. But rather than repress and distort their influence, Socrates detached himself from their power. Such detachment is a central component of a healthy spiritual life.

Detachment

Prior to the birth of my first child, I was fortunate to have had a schedule that allowed me to exercise, work, and meditate on regular basis. I maintained this routine for more than a year leading up to the birth. Although the impending birth did not occupy a great deal of my conscious thought, I felt prepared for the event when it arrived. My wife was also well prepared, having sustained a healthy exercise and diet program for the entire pregnancy. The birth went very well. My wife gave birth without medication after only two hours of hospital labor, and her recovery was swift.

I vividly remember the delivery. With eyes wide open and her head arched upward, it seemed as though my daughter was diving into the oxygenated atmosphere. As a witness to this miraculous event, the only word that I could think of to describe it was "reality." There was no overwhelming feeling of joy or bliss. Just reality stripped of all extraneous concerns. I had never experienced the world with such clarity or intensity. I was fully present to the event and I felt fully alive. I was also relieved that both my wife and daughter were healthy. After my sense of relief waned, it was replaced by a placid and temperate sense of conversion. The conversion was placid and temperate because the circumstances of my reality had changed, not me. Although my reality had just been irreversibly and immeasurably altered, I felt prepared.

This is how I understand detachment. It is not a disconnection or retreat from the world. It is not the repression of emotions. To be detached is to have a clarity and singleness of focus that allows reality to penetrate the depths of consciousness. This is what we referred to in chapter 1 as conscious presence. To be aware of the circumstances of one's life as they occur, to be highly attuned to reality, requires a strong sense of detachment from the powerful and persuasive forces of the emotions. This detachment allows one to become more fully engaged with the world, because misguided thoughts or emotions do not distract a detached consciousness. This is the type of consciousness that Socrates cultivated and sustained throughout his life. He was keenly aware of the issue that mattered most: Always choose right instead of wrong, because ultimately it is the state of one's soul that matters.

Detachment is one of the highest goals on the way to enlightenment in most meditation traditions. One does not meditate to become aloof and disengaged from the world, but to observe the processes of the mind and of the world, so that errant or random thoughts do not lead consciousness astray into fictional perceptions of self and world. The meditative process does not seek to eliminate or deny thoughts or emotions. It seeks to observe them, and to observe from whence they come, so that the attention of consciousness is less vulnerable to their distracting and seductive powers. Hence, one who has achieved a high level of meditative awareness will still experience anger, or joy, or sorrow, but he does not allow the emotion to consume consciousness or generate an impulsive response that he will likely regret.

Although Socrates does not explicitly describe a meditative practice that we can immediately associate with a spiritual pursuit of detachment and enlightenment, he achieved an extremely high level of self-awareness and self-control. He was detached from the world of emotions and had few errant thoughts. This detachment allowed him to perceive reality without distraction and to choose virtue, even in the most extreme circumstances. His detachment allowed him to sustain the highest integrity. Presumably, tragically, it led him to feel the intense pain as a parent who chose to leave behind his family rather than live a life whose virtue was compromised. Fortunately, most parents will never be forced to make such a choice. But Socrates' example provides us with a powerful model to reflect on and integrate into our lives as parents. It reminds us of the importance of integrity, which, along with genuine love, children need and desire most from their parents.

Notes

1. Plato, *Collected Works of Plato*, ed. Edith Hamilton and Huntington Cairns (Princeton, N.J.: Princeton University Press, 1961), 30.

2. Plato, *Collected Works of Plato*, 14.

CHAPTER EIGHT

Discipline

Since I have abandoned organized sports due to age, injuries, and insufficient sleep, my primary mode of exercise is running. At the fifth mile of the six-mile route that I usually run there is a steep hill. Each time that I come to the base of the hill there are two thoughts that occur almost automatically. First I think of the dirt path that awaits me at the top of the hill. After I catch my breath, the path is the most pleasurable part of the run. Beams of sunlight pierce the green canopy of leaves overhead, sporadically illuminating the soft dirt that cushions my strides. The thought of running through the woods on this level, peaceful, secluded path is a little treat that makes the burden of the steep hill I must climb to get there worthwhile.

But I do not harp on this thought. In fact, once I remind myself of the path above, the idea quickly recedes into the back of my mind. Immediately I turn my attention to the individual strides I take to get up the hill. As I run the hill, resistance seems to increase and my body's natural tendency is to tighten up, making each stride more difficult. To counter this tendency, I concentrate on relaxing my body at each step along the way. I try to keep my arms and legs relaxed and my breathing free as I run on the balls of my feet to the top. Using this method to maintain a steady pace up the hill, I derive the most benefit I can from the run. I also manage to minimize the discomfort of overcoming the hill's resistance by concentrating on each stride. At the top, I feel the temporary pain of insufficient oxygen in my lungs as they try to normalize their breathing patterns again. Once the lungs have caught up, I am ready to enjoy the final part of the run on the dirt path.

Recently, while running this stretch, it occurred to me that the methods of concentration that I use to manage the pain and get the most out of my run could be useful for understanding effective parental discipline. The two thoughts that I have at this part of the run (the path above and the individual strides) parallel the necessary elements of good parental discipline: *intention* and *method*. Just as I remind myself of the path that awaits me at the top of the hill, parents who are trying to provide effective discipline to their children must constantly examine the goals they are seeking to achieve with their discipline. As Aristotle reminds us at the outset of the *Nichomachean Ethics*, if there is one good that we desire above all others, and everything we do is a means to achieving that good, knowledge of that good will have a great influence on life.[1]

Following this logic, parents are much more likely to achieve the desired end or purpose of discipline if they hold a clear idea of that end in view. Many would agree with Aristotle that the end we seek to attain for ourselves and for our children is happiness. It is a challenge to maintain a clear vision of what happiness entails. As parents, we must constantly ask what we envision to be the best life for our children, and how we can help them acquire the discipline to achieve that life.

For some, the good life means acquiring the financial status to become a powerful consumer. It means keeping up appearances of success as determined by prevailing social standards. Parents who hold such superficial visions of the good life use methods for helping their children "succeed" that emphasize superficial concerns. For instance, they are likely to push their children to get good grades so that they can get into the best colleges, without being much concerned with whether or not their children's education opens them to new, creative, and genuinely fulfilling ways of living. For these parents, the meaning of life is found in the external rewards of material wealth or social status. Of course this approach usually backfires, unless the child can find insightful guidance and deeper meaning from alternative sources.

Some see in their children an opportunity to relive their own youth, to recapture some of the missed opportunities that passed them by. In doing so, these parents unwittingly sacrifice their children's interests and needs for the sake of their own inane attempts to recapture youth. These visions of the happy life are inadequate to the human spirit. Parents who fail to understand this underestimate or undervalue the genuine needs of their children. Disciplinary methods without an adequate vision of the good life, therefore, are likely to generate resentment in children, because they will interpret such methods as manipulation used to direct them toward goals to which they do not aspire.

Most parents, however, recognize that children must develop their own interests and learn to trust in their own abilities if they are to become well-adjusted, happy adults. If children believe in themselves enough to find and follow what the poet William Blake calls their "firm persuasion"—their passions—and develop the discipline to meet life's necessities and challenges, they are likely to live fulfilling and happy lives. But following my strategy for getting up the hill during my run, I will put the idea of happiness,[2] the goal we seek for our children, in the background and use this chapter to focus on the elements of discipline needed to get there.

Suffering and the Spirit

In the first section of this book, we emphasized the need for parents to achieve high levels of personal development if they are to effectively lead their children to a fulfilling adult life. One of the impediments to such development and to the ability of parents to impart an adequate vision of the good life to their children is their failure to grow and develop along with their children. When this occurs parents tend to see their children as they were when they were infants, dependent and vulnerable. These parents try to protect their children from the world and from the suffering that the world has in store for their children. They try to shelter their children, and in the process they prevent their children from the difficult, sometimes painful, but invaluable learning experiences the world has to offer.

A classic story of this approach to parenting is that of the Buddha, whose father tried to keep him insulated from the world outside the palace walls. He did not want his son to see the suffering and sickness of people on the other side. But curiosity got the better of the child and he escaped from the palace. Outside the gates he saw suffering firsthand. This experience led the Buddha to formulate the first of the four noble truths of Buddhism: There is suffering.

By recognizing that suffering is a basic fact of existence, Buddhism invites us to face our difficulties rather than hide from them. Since suffering and the problems that lead to suffering are inevitable, we ought to concentrate on alleviating them rather than denying that they exist. This is an important lesson for parents. Children will face problems and suffering in their lives. This is a fact. Responsible parents therefore prepare their children to deal with their suffering rather than trying to insulate them from it. They exemplify and teach the discipline to endure discomfort and pain in difficult situations. They do not run away from problems but face up to them. Armed with such experience, children, like their parents ahead of them, can overcome suffering rather than avoid it. The dynamic of accepting short-term pain or discomfort in order to overcome difficult situations is not only the central tenet of good discipline; it is the age-old formula for spiritual growth. Such growth is at the heart of human fulfillment, and it requires the discipline to put aside what is familiar and comfortable and take on what is new, strange, or difficult. The poet T. S. Eliot succinctly describes this process in the *Four Quartets*. He writes:

> In order to arrive there,
> To arrive where you are, to get from where you are
>   not,
>   You must go by the way in which there is no ecstasy.
> In order to arrive at what you do not know
>   You must go by a way which is the way of ignorance.
> In order to possess what you do not possess
>   You must go by the way of dispossession.
> In order to arrive at what you are not
>   You must go through the way in which you are not. [3]

In this passage Eliot is describing the movement that is necessary to get to where we want to be, to a place in which we experience the highest fulfillment or happiness. The passage implies that we are not yet there. The journey we must take to get there is often without a map ("the way of ignorance"). This is difficult ("there is no ecstasy"), since it requires giving up what is familiar and comfortable for what is unknown. But it is necessary if we are to experience genuine spiritual growth.

In this passage Eliot is echoing a point that is central to all of the great wisdom traditions. Jesus tells his followers they must leave their family behind if they are to follow him. The Buddha had to jettison the life of privilege and pleasure to find enlightenment. Socrates describes the authentic philosophical life as a process of practicing dying, practicing death each day.

Balance

For each of these monumental figures, the movement of spiritual health is a movement away from the familiar and into the unknown or unfamiliar. The most puzzling description of this movement is that of the philosopher who must constantly practice dying. What does it mean to practice dying? To understand Socrates here is to gain valuable insight into the discipline that is necessary for authentic spiritual growth. One way of interpreting Socrates' description of the philosophical life is to draw on the insights of twentieth-century psychology and the phenomenon of the ego. For most of us, our ego-identity is the self-image that is formed by the environments in which we are raised and live. It is the image of ourselves that we acquire through the opinions, descriptions, and attitudes that others project onto us. In turn, it is the image that we portray to the external world around us. This image is fragile. We spend a great deal of energy protecting and fortifying it. Whether it is children wanting to fit in with the group or adults trying to impress their neighbors, the ego-self seeks acceptance through praise and honor, which are its nourishment for survival.

This is the part of the self that Socrates wants to kill each day. Of course in order to practice the death of the ego, there must be a healthy sense of self below and beyond the ego-self. As long as the ego-self is integrated into the whole self in a healthy way, as long as we recognize the need for a healthy ego along with its limits, we can then work on getting beyond the restrictions it places on the spirit. The interplay between the ego and its limits is what M. Scott Peck calls balance, which is one of the four moments of discipline he identifies in his classic work, *The Road Less Traveled*.

Socrates recognizes that we must be able to get beyond the ego's tendency to cling to material things or frivolous praise if we are to discover a more spiritually healthy and fulfilled self. To practice dying is to forgo the ego's desires for what is familiar and self-serving. This requires discipline. It may be as simple as passing up dessert because the immediate gratification of the sweet taste undermines the overall health that the self desires. It may mean examining the state of one's soul in silence instead of running to the mall to spend last week's paycheck. For parents it means resisting the inclination to lose patience with a sick child whose crying seems endless. It may involve designating a room to which family members retreat when angry, rather than lashing out on every impulse. Essentially Socrates is telling us to sacrifice the interests of the small (ego) self in order to achieve a more fulfilled, higher self. This is the central dynamic of self-discipline that is at the heart of all great spiritual traditions. Nowhere is it more essential than in parenting.

Peck points out that "when we teach ourselves and our children discipline, we are teaching them and ourselves how to suffer and also how to grow."[4] We do not grow spiritually if we hide from problems, suffering, and pain. Spiritual growth and maturity, which are prerequisites for happiness, are the primary point of discipline. The ability to face one's problems and endure suffering for the sake of spiritual growth is the most precious gift parents can give to their children. Such growth is the goal, the path at the top of the steep hill, that we all must climb day after day in order to achieve a healthy mind and body.

Self-Examination

This is not an easy climb, especially for parents who are under the constant pressure of increasing bills, demanding children, and their own fatigue. On a recent summer night, as my wife and I were getting the children ready for bed, Caitriona began to cry, saying that she had an earache. She had been swimming the previous days and it was possible that the water combined with air-conditioning had led to an earache. On the other hand, Caitriona, who is four, never before had had an earache. The infections that she gets almost always settle in her throat in various forms of coughs. As the night progressed, her disposition deteriorated quickly. She was soon crying hysterically, still complaining about her ear. Since it was late and she had been playing hard for a few days in a row, she was also exhausted. As most parents know, a child will rarely attribute sadness or discomfort to tiredness.

Unfortunately, my wife was also exhausted. She had had little sleep the previous night and had been with the children all day. Her patience had worn thin. As Caitriona's discomfort and crying escalated, my wife began to express her frustration with having a pediatrician in Manhattan who is very difficult to get on the phone at times like this. She wanted someone who she could go to immediately, to get an antibiotic and eliminate the problem. She needed sleep and she wanted to alleviate Caitriona's discomfort.

Although she was in no mood for a conversation, I reminded her that one of the reasons we chose our pediatrician is that we do not want our children's bodies ravaged by unnecessary antibiotics. The guiding principle of our pediatrician is that the body will overcome most ailments on its own. We can foster that process with natural remedies that do not harm the body. Also, because he gives us extensive notes and explanations of what he does, we often know how to help the children when ailments arise. My wife was tired and didn't want to hear it. But I remembered the remedy for ear infections and went to the medicine cabinet to get the tea tree oil.

Once we had figured out a way to address the problem, my wife felt much better. I warmed the oil and got some cotton to dispense it into Caitriona's ear. There was one problem; Caitriona did not want any part of it, and became even more hysterical when she saw me coming with the oil. This confirmed for me that she was more tired than sick. She is usually very good about taking medicine that she needs. My suggestion, which we followed, was to put Caitriona to bed. She was asleep in minutes. The next morning she was fine and we were reassured about our approach to caring for our children's health.

Looking back on the previous night, we realized that my wife's fatigue and the frustration that resulted caused a temporary lapse in discipline. She was too tired to address the situation in the way that she usually does, and there was a part of her that wanted a quick fix. On the surface, the goal that we sought in this case was easy to define; we wanted Caitriona to be healthy. But we momentarily disagreed about how to achieve that goal: antibiotics, tea tree oil, or sleep. A more careful scrutiny of the source of our disagreement, however, revealed that the goal that we sought was not as simple as it first appeared. My wife was exhausted. She needed to sleep. She wanted Caitriona to be better, but she wanted it in the quickest way possible so that she could meet her needs. Her need for sleep, though valid, caused her to want to overcome the pain of the situation with antibiotics. In a clearer state of mind antibiotics would have been a last resort. We learned that even the most disciplined parent can have lapses of judgment in difficult situations.

This episode reminded us of the constant need for vigilant self-examination. Only by carefully examining our lives can we understand the motivations behind our decisions. Only by carefully examining the complex motivations affecting our decisions can we act in accordance with our own principles and take control of our own lives.

Parents are faced with such difficult choices daily. A child cries for candy. Do we give in and let the child have it to end the crying, or do we hold our ground even if the child makes a scene? The decisions we make are always a matter of circumstance, and we need good judgment to navigate the choices we face. But the judgment we bring to a situation is a function of our self-discipline. The extent to which we have developed the techniques and capacity for accepting pain and discomfort and working through them will determine our ability to make good choices. My wife suffered because our daughter was uncomfortable. Her empathic suffering was compounded by her own discomfort due to exhaustion. Her weariness led her to momentarily lapse into a longing to solve the problem in the way that most parents we know would have solved it. In a sense she was longing for what was familiar. But such a lapse would involve abdicating our ability to solve the problem. Even if it were a minor infection, a traditional doctor would likely have prescribed antibiotics, which would solve the immediate problem but also ravage her body in the process. Such a decision would have led us to forgo all of our research and the information that we learned from our pediatrician (not to mention the money spent to get that information) for a quick fix that we really didn't want for Caitriona.

The desire for a quick fix to avoid suffering or discomfort is not unusual in the relationship between parent and children. What parent hasn't given in to a child who is crying for a treat that he would rather she didn't have? And yet it is in these seemingly insignificant exchanges that discipline is exercised by the parent and learned by the child. In resisting the pleas of a crying child for the sake of the child's well-being, we endure the discomfort of listening to the crying. But such endurance, simple as it is, provides important lessons to the child. It teaches the child that her parent is willing to suffer through an uncomfortable situation for a better long-term outcome. It also teaches the child that not every wish will be granted in life. The world is going to resist his individual will. Gratification must be postponed if one is to achieve the good things in life rather than what is immediately satisfying. In a world that is addicted to immediate gratification, to be able to delay gratification is an essential part of a disciplined life. In thinking about the importance of having the ability to delay gratification, I am reminded of a contemporary Native American leader who says that unlike the mainstream of American society, which seems addicted to immediate gratification, his people are willing to wait hundreds of years for their prayers to be answered.

Of course we must be careful in speaking about teaching our children the skill of delayed gratification. In *The Drama of the Gifted Child*, Alice Miller provides solemn examples of parents who devastate their children, causing lasting pain under the guise of discipline and delayed gratification. Miller calls our attention to the powerful tendency to repeat hurtful patterns of behavior. Rather than face the humiliation that we suffered as children, we unconsciously avenge that pain on our own children. We see the humiliation we suffered in the eyes of our children and avert our pain by exercising our power over our children. Miller shares her observations of a couple and their child, who whined for one of the ice-cream sticks each parent had. Both refused to give him their ice cream, telling him that it was too cold for him, while laughing at his display of discontent. This caused him to cry more, and when they were finished the father handed him the empty stick. The child licked it and then threw it away. He looked at it again as if to pick it up but left it on the ground. Miller surmises that the child was not upset because of an unsatisfied oral fixation. She saw a child who was hurt and frustrated. "His wish to hold the ice-cream stick in his hand like the others was not understood. Worse still, it was laughed at; they made fun of his wish. He was faced with two giants who supported each other and who were proud of being consistent while he, quite alone in his distress, could say nothing beyond 'no.' Nor could he make himself clear to his parents with his gestures (though they were very expressive). He had no advocate."[5] To help us understand this scene, Miller asks the following crucial questions: Why did these parents behave with so little empathy? Why didn't they think of giving him the stick with a little ice cream on it? Why did they both stand there laughing, showing so little concern for the child's distress? It was not because they were cold and unkind parents, according to Miller, but because they too were insecure children in grown-up bodies cloaked with the authority of parenthood. It is likely that their own childhood insecurities had never been resolved. It was much easier to avoid these insecurities in solidarity with each other than to confront them in the vulnerability of their child. If they had had the self-awareness and courage to confront their own unresolved pain from childhood, they would have been willing to explore the child's feelings. Rather than lock arms in solidarity with each other against the child, they would have recognized the child's wants and needs. They would have seen that he needed to feel a part of the group by holding and tasting the ice cream, as they were doing. If that was out of the question, he needed to know that his parents knew how he felt, rather than be dismissed with laughter.

Miller's analysis of the unconscious inheritance of patterns of behavior reiterates the essential need for vigilant self-examination. Not only is the unexamined life not worth living, as Socrates tells us, the unexamined life of parents is a sure formula for passing on devastating hurt to our children. The value of a disciplined life is nowhere more urgent than in parenting. Disciplined parents need to examine and understand the unconscious patterns of behavior that we inherit from past generations if we are to protect our children from hurtful patterns of behavior. We must become aware of the pain that these patterns have caused us in childhood, because it is only by recognizing this pain, and suffering through it, that we can break the patterns and condemn them unequivocally.

Teaching Discipline

While Miller's analysis in invaluable for understanding the danger of unconscious patterns of behavior in parents, it does not tell the whole story of what we inherit from our parents. It is certain that the patterns of behavior that parents demonstrate are imprinted on the child's psyche from the earliest days of infancy. These patterns shape the contents of the child's unconscious and hence his orientation to the world for the remainder of his life. But it is not the case that this inheritance is always only a source of pain and humiliation. While it may be inevitable that parents cause their children the greatest hurt they are likely to ever experience, many also provide their children with the discipline—that is, the psychological, moral, and intellectual resources—that is necessary for overcoming their hurt and many of life's obstacles. Just as we receive negative imprints from our parent's patterns of behavior, we also receive positive ones.

I was reminded of this fact recently as I drove down the New Jersey Turnpike on my way to work in Newark, New Jersey. Anyone who has made this drive or who has visited Newark knows that it is economically, aesthetically, and environmentally impoverished. At the school where I was teaching, there was a heightened security alert because of the high rate of crime in the area. One day as I headed toward this unpleasant destination, I felt a tinge of self-pity raising its timid head. Thankfully I am experienced enough to know that to wallow in such feelings never makes things easier and usually makes them worse. The easy antidote to self-pity is to think of those around us who have a much more difficult life.

In summoning this antidote, I did not have to think of strangers. I thought of my father and his journey as an Irish immigrant. He too spent time working in Newark, as a carpenter. He also worked all over Manhattan, often carrying a heavy toolbox on and off the subway. He went to jobs that were full of filth, with no heat in the winter and no air-conditioning in the summer. He endured the profane comments and conversations of the less refined personalities often found on construction sights. He tackled jobs that seemed insurmountable at the start. He never gave us a speech about what it takes to be successful. He showed us.

As children, my brothers and I learned the patterns of a workday. I watched my father leave for the subway every morning around six and return home around four o'clock. We would have dinner when he got home and then play ball or do homework. When we got older we worked with him, not only learning the skills of the trade, but the discipline of going to work every day. He demonstrated a steely resolve to solve problems that seemed unsolvable, in the most difficult of circumstances. (We recently renovated a house together that had been abandoned for almost ten years. The roof had a large hole. Under the hole the second floor had rotted and was partially collapsed onto the first floor. The clothes and belongings of the last people to live in the house were scattered all over, also rotting. In the midst of this apparent chaos, my father not only had a detailed plan of how to proceed from the beginning of the job until the end, he found and removed numerous animals that had died in the house. Of course, one could not stand by without helping. We all got a chance to remove a dead raccoon or two.) And here I was traveling to an air-conditioned office to talk about my greatest passion: the ideas of philosophy. My self-pity was replaced with feelings of gratitude for the positive patterns of behavior that I inherited from my parents. I realized that these patterns of behavior are just as powerful and just as important as the hurtful ones. It is by example that these patterns are most effectively passed on to our children.

Sensitivity and Time

Although parents' primary mode of teaching children the skills of discipline is modeling patterns of behavior, parents also have the responsibility of making disciplinary decisions on a daily basis. Children regularly reach out for disciplinary guidance. In order to recognize these pleas from our children, we must be sensitive to their disciplinary needs. Such sensitivity can be achieved only by spending sufficient amounts of time with our children.

This is not always easy. Parents need time alone and time with each other. They need time to think and time to work. For me, since I do most of my work at home, it is often frustrating to hear the crying and fighting between my daughters. The most difficult issue is bedtime. From the first weeks of her life, Caitriona was coddled to sleep. Like many first-time parents, we jumped to her every moan. Our hypersensitivity was often justified, since she was colicky for a couple of months. But we created a set of expectations on her part that remain with her four years later. As she grew into her toddler years, we hoped that she would begin to feel more comfortable going to bed without one of us staying with her until she fell asleep. But she is a strong-willed girl and she was not giving in.

I used to sometimes allow myself to get frustrated by her demands, especially if I had work to be done, or if my wife and I had something important to discuss. But as Caitriona's resolve remained, I found that her need for bedtime company no longer frustrated me. In fact, I came to look forward to this time with her. The change in my attitude came about one night when I asked her why she didn't like to go to bed alone. She told me about the monsters that were outside the dark window and in her imagination. These monsters scared her. Not wanting to discredit her feelings or the workings of her imagination, I asked her what the monsters looked like. She gave me some details of their color and size (though the details changed as the story progressed). I then suggested the possibility that they were nice monsters. She thought about it for a moment and agreed that it was possible, but they still scared her. I assured her that even if I had to go downstairs while she was sleeping, I would not let the monsters hurt her or her sister. She rolled over and went to sleep.

After that night, I recognized the importance of quiet, intimate time that enables us to pray and talk for a while. I think that had I reacted out of frustration to her refusal to go to bed on her own, I would never have known about the real fear she has of the dark. She would never have expressed that fear and it would have festered inside her consciousness until it emerged into something else. I now know that it is during that half hour or so before she goes to sleep that I can learn about what is on her mind. I can learn her fears and her concerns. Every once in a while I am treated to something hilarious.

One night she lay completely silent for more than a half hour, apparently rehearsing scenes from that day in her mind; then she suddenly turned to face me. Looking me directly in the eyes, as if she were about to reveal a deep, dark secret, she said, "Daddy. Kitty (her saintly grandmother) said, 'Fuck it. Oh Jesus,' when Eilish (her cousin) missed the ball in her soccer game." (Her grandmother denies this account of what she said.) Caitriona said nothing else. She just rolled back over and went off to sleep, as I bit my lip to hold in my laughter.

Of course there are no guarantees that parents will know what is bothering their children deep inside. But by spending intimate time with them, we can better recognize and address their pleas for guidance and direct them away from situations and behavior that require major interventions later on. Like the runner who focuses on each step along the way, parents are likely to minimize children's fears and pain by attending to the details of their lives as often as possible and with real concern and sensitivity. Dramatic attempts to steer children right after their minor pleas have been unmet over a long period of time are often made too late and rarely have the desired effect. At best they can make a child recognize the pain he must work through to acquire the disciplinary skills needed to live a self-reliant and fulfilling life. It is my hope that by spending this time with Caitriona, I can be more sensitive to what she is thinking, and by listening intently to her, convince her that what she feels and thinks is important. In this way, we can address minor concerns before they become major concerns.

This time also gives us a chance to rectify disagreements and misunderstandings that may have occurred during the day. Even the most sensitive and patient parents say and do inappropriate things to our children. It is important, I think, to let them know that we are aware of our mistakes. In this way, they learn that it is acceptable to make their own mistakes, and that, when they do, it is honorable to apologize for doing so. By bringing these hidden concerns to the surface, we gain greater control over our emotions and feelings. In turn, we become more aware of what motivates us to act and think as we do. This awareness is an essential element in self-discipline and in effectively disciplining our children.

Discipline and Morality

At the outset of this discussion of discipline, I suggested that there are two major concerns in practicing good parental discipline: intention and method. In other words, what is our goal and how do we achieve it? The primary goal of good parental discipline is to prepare children to be responsible citizens who are capable of living healthy and fulfilling lives by trusting in their abilities and by following their passions with firm persuasion. We have emphasized the psychological dimension of discipline and the need for self-examination. We have also pointed to the importance of being sensitive to the needs of children, especially those needs that are not immediately obvious. To conclude this chapter, I want to point out one other essential need of children that is often overshadowed by psychological concerns. This is the need for moral discipline and moral intelligence. In *The Moral Intelligence of Children*, psychiatrist Robert Coles makes it clear that children learn how to be with other people by watching how their parents are with each other and with other people, not by memorizing ethical arguments. He writes, "the child is a witness; the child is an ever-attentive witness of grown-up morality—or lack thereof; the child looks and looks for cues as to how one ought to behave and finds them galore as we parents and teachers go about our lives. . . ."[6] In this passage Coles reaffirms our point that children learn by imitating what they see adults doing. But in addressing the moral life of children, Coles is bringing to the forefront a basic issue that many parents and adults in general tend to overlook: the concern for the moral life of our children.

Too often the moral life of our children gets conflated with the psychological. It is a strong temptation for parents to justify bad behavior with psychological explanations. It is true that children who behave immorally on a consistent basis are usually doing so out of deep psychological pain. It is important to uncover the source of such children's pain in an attempt to alleviate it and redirect their behavior. But it is also the case that bad behavior needs to be identified as such. Children need to learn right from wrong and good from bad. While we are all too willing to praise children for mediocre behavior and accomplishments, we have grown timid when it comes to punishing bad behavior. This imbalance leads to moral confusion on the part of children. As Plato points out in the *Republic*, it is a benefit to one who commits an immoral or unjust act to be punished; otherwise his soul will fall out of balance. Parents who are unwilling to punish their children are sending their children incomplete and often confusing messages. If children learn that there are no consequences for wrongdoing early on in life, they will have a hard time adjusting when they meet the disapproval of others later on.

Therefore, as a part of parents' responsibility to prepare their children to be well-adjusted adults, they must make it clear which type of behavior is acceptable and which is not.

There are strong philosophical precedents to justify the use of punishment as a tool for effective parenting. For eighteenth-century German philosopher Georg Wilhelm Hegel and twentieth-century American philosopher Charles Sanders Peirce, the basic structure of reality is triadic. That is, all things that come to be have three component parts or movements. We can refer to these three parts simply as firstness, secondness, and thirdness. The category of firstness refers to the blind impulsive drive in beings to forge forth into the world via self-expression. This urge or drive is in every living thing, and it is evident in human infants as their cries demand that their needs be met. Firstness by itself is without definition or individuation. It does not experience itself as anything unique because it has never been differentiated from others in the world. It is only by encountering opposition to one's self that one can begin to establish an identity or awareness as someone or something different from others.

The category of secondness exists in opposition to the self-expression of firstness. Secondness interrupts the blind, unreflective willfulness of firstness. For children, this occurs when a parent denies a child's request. The child begins to understand that the world is not at his command. To hear the word "no," to be denied, is the beginning of an awareness for the child that there are others in the world with their own needs and desires. The world will not always grant him his wishes. In fact, the world will often present obstacles to one's willful desires.

As a result of the encounter between firstness and secondness, a higher, more developed plane of existence is achieved. Firstness adapts to the opposition of secondness and a new identity is formed. The new identity is aware of others and their needs. It understands that there are limits to what it can do and hope for. It understands itself as an individual that is separate from others and not just an impulsive drive for self-expression. This higher state of development, being, or consciousness is thirdness.

When my daughters are exhausted and crying for no other reason than the fact that they are tired, it is often counterproductive to reason with them. Their tiredness makes it impossible for them to reason with me, and so they continue to feel miserable regardless of what explanations or concessions are made. I look on these moments as if the children are stuck in firstness. They are expressing their discomfort, and their discomfort will not allow them to feel or express anything else. The discomfort takes over their being, and they are incapable of realizing other ways of feeling or thinking. They are also blind to the needs and sometimes even the presence of others. At these times, I often hold one of my daughters firmly against my body while walking around the house, so that she becomes conscious of something other than her state of misery. At first she tries to squirm and push herself away, but I hold her tight. After realizing that she cannot go anywhere, that she cannot just express herself in any way that she wants, she calms down. Her crying eases, and the firm clasp is subtly transformed into a hug. This is not punishment exactly, but it is an example of inserting oneself as secondness to resist and oppose the child as firstness. The end result, the third, is a calmer, more peaceful child.

This model can be extended to address the moral development of children. As children grow and seek to impose their will on the world, they will inevitably come up against opposition. As parents, it is our responsibility to provide opposition in the appropriate ways at the appropriate times. By inserting ourselves regularly, consistently, and compassionately, we allow children to begin to form their own moral conscience. By condemning the swiping of a doll each time it is done, for instance, we teach the child that she cannot just take things from others. She learns that there are personal boundaries that must be respected. By punishing such behavior when an explanation is repeatedly ignored, by expressing disappointment in words or actions, we teach children the types of behavior that are acceptable and unacceptable. By making children aware of the invasiveness of such an action we cause them to realize that it is wrong and that they would not like it if done to them. In other words, we begin to teach them the value and meaning of the Golden Rule: Treat others as you would have them treat you. This principle of moral behavior is very difficult for children to appropriate if parents do not provide the boundaries to make them aware that they must coexist with others in the world. Hence parents must discipline their children with an eye toward moral principles. This sometimes involves serving as the opposition to their blind impulse to express their own drives and satisfy their own desires.

Effective discipline is hard work for parents. There are many issues of which one must be cognizant. Parents are called to be sensitive but firm, compassionate but convinced. This takes time and patience. It demands that parents hold the moral development of their children in high regard. It also requires parents to clarify the values that they want to live by and pass on to their children. This is not an easy task in a world that seems oblivious to moral values and the good life to which they contribute. But good parenting is not a mainstream activity. Good parents will often find themselves working against the tide of the modern world. But good parents also understand that this is their most important task, for their children are their greatest legacy.

Notes

1. Aristotle, *Nichomachean Ethics*, in *The Basic Works of Aristotle*, 935.

2. See chapter 2 for a detailed discussion of happiness.

3. T. S. Eliot, *The Four Quartets* (New York: Harcourt, Brace, Jovanovich, 1971), 29.

4. M. Scott Peck, *The Road Less Traveled: A New Psychology of Love, Traditional Values, and Spiritual Growth* (New York: Simon and Schuster, 1978), 17.

5. Miller, *The Drama of the Gifted Child*, 71.

6. Robert Coles, *The Moral Intelligence of Children* (New York: Random House, 1977), 5.

CHAPTER NINE

Higher Love

Over the fifteen years that I have been reading, writing, and teaching philosophy, one of the most important, provocative, and challenging thinkers that I have encountered is the twentieth-century French phenomenologist Emmanuel Levinas. There are two distinct qualities in Levinas's work from which the major challenges arise. One is Levinas's language. To articulate his philosophy, Levinas is forced to use conventional philosophical terms in unconventional ways. To make sense of Levinas, at least initially, one must wrestle with almost every sentence to decipher the meaning that he is trying to bring forth. But Levinas's language is not a mere stylistic flaw. His style is necessitated by the radical task of his philosophy. He is trying to get beyond what he perceives to be fundamental and fatal errors endemic to the entire philosophical tradition of the West. But to do so, he must use the terminology of that tradition. As a result, we find Levinas twisting and bending the language, forcing the reader to reencounter familiar terms in unfamiliar ways. Thus to understand Levinas, the reader must allow himself to be taken in by the texts. That is, the reader must be willing to trust in Levinas's positions and suspend belief in his ordinary understanding of the self, its goals, and its relationship to the world.

I hope to spare you, the reader, from the difficulty of Levinas's language. It is the second challenge of his work from which I do not intend to protect you, but rather lead you to feel its full force. This challenge arises out of the extremely high standards of ethics that Levinas uncovers in his phenomenological account of human relationships. I know of no other thinker who sets the standards of ethics so high. These standards challenge and disturb even the highest virtues and truths that other philosophers have articulated and sought to achieve. In fact, Levinas sets the bar so high, many wonder if it is feasible for human beings to ever meet it. And yet, when I examine the relationship between parents and their children, I see some of the most central and difficult elements of Levinas's ethics being lived out on a daily basis. One purpose of this chapter then is to present the central insights in Levinas's ethics as a means to better understand the highest, most difficult, and most fulfilling aspects of the relationship between parents and children. And in the process, we will identify for parents what they already intuitively know about the higher love they share with their children.

The Face

In *Amazing Grace: A Vocabulary of Faith*, best-selling author Kathleen Norris tells a story about a baby she noticed while passing through an airport. She writes:

> The baby was staring intently at other people, and as soon as he recognized a human face, no matter whose it was, no matter if it was young or old, pretty or ugly, bored or happy or worried-looking he would respond with absolute delight. It was beautiful to see. Our drab departure gate had become the gate of heaven. And as I watched that baby play with any adult who would allow it, I felt as awe-struck as Jacob, because I realized that this is how God looks at us, staring into our faces in order to be delighted, to see the creature he made and called good, along with the rest of creation.[1]

Unfettered by the weight of adult anxiety and responsibility, the infant indiscriminately welcomes all who care to look into his eyes. The infant is delighted by the presence of others, without judgment and without compromise, regardless of their physical appearance. With uncanny spiritual perceptiveness and poetic grace, Norris suggests that God and the infant look on others in the same way. In the nonjudgmental gaze of the infant, Norris sees a trace of God.

Levinas also sees the trace of God in the face, not just in the face of innocent infants, but in the face of all human beings. For Levinas, the human face is a trace or gateway to an awesome, infinite, incomprehensible reality that stops us in our tracks if we allow ourselves to become engaged by it. Most of the time, we are unmoved by the true, deep reality of the face because we are preoccupied with our own concerns. But when we welcome the face of another human being, without preconceived ideas about who or what it is, like the infant does, we are thrown into a realm of human experience that is different from our everyday experience. This other realm of experience is what Levinas calls the ethical.

In the ethical relation the face-to-face encounter is not symmetrical. It is not a meeting of two free and equal beings. In fact, if I open myself to the other, I experience such complexity and depth behind the visage of the face that I am unable to comprehend or conceptualize the other with my rational, thinking mind. The complexity and depth of the other overwhelms the rational, conceptual mind. By overwhelming me in this way, the other not only calls my individual freedom into question, but shatters the ego's sense of self and renders it temporarily ineffective. As a result, the self's ordinary orientation toward the other is interrupted. The concerns that constitute its everyday identity are set aside. With a shattered sense of self, unable to make sense of the other through ordinary thought, the self is humbled by the presence of the other.

Although the everyday ego-self is put out of commission in the ethical encounter with the face of the other, all is not lost. With the everyday concerns that usually occupy our minds temporarily suspended in the face of the other, we discover a part of ourselves that is deeper or more fundamental to who we are. In place of the everyday sense of self, the ethical encounter with the other reveals an inescapable, indelible feeling of obligation for the other. Like the spontaneous delight that the infant experiences in the face of the other, the feeling of obligation that one experiences on encountering and opening to the human face is preconscious or prerational. Unlike the infant, however, the adult experiences an inescapable sense of responsibility toward the other in the fallout from being overwhelmed by the face. This responsibility, according to Levinas, is the most basic, most primordial experience of human life. Just as the infant identifies with, and delights in, the presence of others before he gains a sense of self, below and prior to our adult concerns in the everyday world, we have an indelible responsibility to care for the other's well-being. In fact, it is when the interests and concerns of everyday life are referred back to or connected with this responsibility that they find their deepest meaning.

I think I know what Levinas means when he says that the face of the other breaks through our everyday consciousness and concerns. Before I had children I was an excellent sleeper. Post-children, my ability for sleeping well has disintegrated severely. I often lay awake for hours thinking about the best schools for our children, or a lecture I am giving the next day. Sometimes I even stay awake in anticipation of being woken by our infant son, who will need to be fed. When he does wake and I stumble out of bed, I am often cranky or feeling self-pity, thinking that I will be too tired to perform well the next day. And yet, there has never been a night, when I arrive at his crib and look down on his beautiful face, when all displeasure does not dissipate instantly. When I lift his tiny body and hold the silky soft skin of his face against mine, my stumbling steps are transformed into deliberate, care-filled, meditative strides. As I hold him in my arms and feed him, there are no more anxiety-ridden thoughts. After the bottle is finished and he has made his obligatory last burp, I (usually) fall off to sleep, having been relieved of my mental burdens. James' face, like a magic balm, soothes my soul almost every night. The vision of his face truly does break through my ego-centered thoughts and concerns. When it does, I not only acknowledge the infinite obligation I have to care for him, I revel in it.

For Levinas, the obligation we have toward (every) other is an essential and indelible characteristic of human nature. But he realizes that it is most often forgotten or overshadowed by the concerns and interests of the ego-self. The ego-self dominates human consciousness in order to meet the demands of everyday life and to exercise its sense of freedom. The freedom to pursue one's interests (e.g., sleep) and to meet the demands of everyday life constitutes the realm of the same, or of economy. In this realm, need generates the movement of the ego-self.

Motivations and Meaning for the Ego-Self

At the time that I was a graduate student in New York, my younger brother and a friend from our neighborhood were studying in San Francisco. San Francisco is an ideal city in which to have friends if one has the time to visit and minimal responsibilities. As a graduate student, I had spare time and few responsibilities. So I took full advantage of my brother's and his friend's hospitality. At the time, we were hanging on to some of the customs of the Irish American neighborhood in which we grew up. On some nights this entailed drinking more than we needed.

This policy backfired on me during one visit. We enjoyed a lively night at a few taverns around the city. The next day arrived with all of the symptoms of having forgotten to pay attention to intake volume. I did my best to stay focused on the Van Morrison concert that we were going to that night. But my body kept reminding me of my carelessness of the previous night. As we walked around the city under a hot sun, there was little I could do to feel better. Burdened with insufficient sleep and hydration, along with the standard tinge of depression to which alcohol treats its users, I felt and expressed numerous needs, one after the other, to my companions. For most of the day, they were so tolerant of my narcissism that I failed to realize I was constantly telling them what I needed, whether it was a drink, food, or sleep. Finally, after accommodating my childish narcissism for most of the day, my friend's patience was exhausted. He didn't overreact but merely stated, in a playful and direct way, "I never met someone with as many needs as you have." Instantly, I snapped out of my self-absorbed state and apologized.

My behavior on that sickly day is a rather extreme example of the ego-self and its incessant needs. While my self-absorbed narcissism was more pronounced due to the state of health I was in, most of us rely on a subtle but strong dose of narcissistic self-interest in our everyday lives. Because our society places such a high priority on individual rights and freedoms, much of our attention and energy is devoted to establishing a firm identity for the self. Armed with a sense of self that we present to the world, we seek to meet or exceed the standards and approval of society. We fortify the identity of the ego-self by satisfying its needs. This usually involves choosing significant tasks and working to accomplish them. The process of fulfilling needs by choosing a task, working to meet that task, and accomplishing the task constitutes what Levinas calls the realm of the same or the realm of economy.

In this realm, our lives derive meaning from the tasks that we choose and pursue. For instance, most of my students focus on achieving high grades and earning their degree. For four years, this is their primary concern, and it provides their lives with meaning and purpose. As they move toward their final year, their attention begins to shift toward finding a job and the amount of money they will be paid. Once they leave college and begin working, they choose new goals to pursue, such as saving money for a house or a car. Levinas appropriately calls this the realm of the same, because in this realm all of one's pursuits are generated from the ego-self and ultimately refer back to the self. That which is encountered along the way to achieving one's goals is appropriated into the ego-self's conceptual horizon or field of concern. Within this horizon, the ego-self analyzes, evaluates, and judges what is useful in the pursuit of its goals and what is not. If it determines that something is useful, it brings it into its horizon of understanding. If it deems something not useful, it disregards it or transforms it to make it useful. In any case, within the realm of the same the other is never treated as other. It is never encountered as it is in itself, but only through the mediation of the ego-self's needs, interests, and conceptual horizon.

We need to take this realm of experience seriously in order to survive. The ego must be developed to have healthy self-esteem if one is to choose and fulfill the goals that are conducive to the best life. It is the ego-self and its ability to analyze, comprehend, and judge the world that enables us to meet the demands of everyday life. This is not to be condemned.

The danger we face in meeting these demands, however, is the tendency to allow our attention to become completely absorbed by the interests and needs of the ego-self while ignoring the ethical obligations that persist beneath these interests. Given the intense pressure that modern society places on individuality, rights, freedom, and self-expression, it is not surprising to see so many live as though the everyday needs and interests of the ego were all there is to one's life. Many fail to find any meaning or value beyond the goals they choose and the rewards that accompany their achievement. If this happens, one becomes trapped in a narcissistic world constituted exclusively of self-interest. Life becomes a cyclical pattern of satisfying needs for those things we lack, only to create more needs. In this process life has purpose, though it is, ultimately, an empty and unfulfilling purpose.

In the everyday world, which is dominated by self-interests, the catalyst for movement or activity is need. Needs arise out of that which we lack, and through work we try to alleviate those needs. When we are hungry, we cook food to satisfy that hunger. When we are tired, we need sleep, so we go to bed. When we want more expensive goods, we seek a higher-paying job or work more hours to be able to afford them. The activity and/or the goods that accompany the activity satisfy the need. For many, the meaning and purpose of life is found in the creation and fulfillment of new needs. But such meaning is cut off from the most purposeful and profound dimension of human experience: desire for the other.

A Woman's Movement

Along with civil rights and the environmental movement, the most influential movement in the United States over the past thirty years has been the women's movement. Feminist thinkers and activists have forged new ground and new opportunities for women in every sector of society. While there is still work to be done to achieve equality, safety, and respect, women are now running multinational corporations and small businesses. There are an increasing number of female professionals in fields that were traditionally dominated by men. Women wield the highest levels of power in political life and compete with professional male athletes for the public's attention.

Along with all of these accomplishments, another telling sign of the movement's success is the fact that many women who do not consider themselves activists or feminists participate in careers and activities that continue to advance the movement. By meeting the highest standards of performance, women are forcing society to take notice of their talents and provide the appropriate compensations and acknowledgments.

One such woman I know worked full-time to pay her way through school. After working late into the night, she would study before going to sleep and again early in the morning. She graduated at the top of her class. She was hired by a leading accounting firm in New York City, where she worked twelve to fourteen hour days before moving on to a private firm. She quickly ascended the ranks in the new firm, and managed a department of twenty accountants before she was twenty-seven years old. In addition to supervising the work of those in her department, she traveled around the country to consult with managers in other branches of the company. For all of this work, she was paid handsomely and was on her way to greater success in her field.

In the context of Levinas's thought, this woman was flourishing in the realm of economy. She was taking advantage of her talents and her freedom to choose rewarding career paths. As she ascended the levels of her corporation, her influence grew. The increases in money that she was earning provided her with greater freedom to buy and invest. Within the realm of economy, she was a real success. Like that of so many other women, her success solidified and advanced opportunities for all women.

But also like many other women who enjoy success within the realm of economy, she was not fully satisfied with her life. She wanted a family. She made a courageous decision to leave her career behind and devote herself to full-time motherhood. As bright and capable as she was in her professional career, it could not prepare her for all of the adjustments she would have to make to be a good mother. She was going from a world that demanded attention to detail, precision, and efficiency into a world in which things are messy and unpredictable. At the end of each day of work, she could evaluate a project and organize the steps needed to complete it. There was always a clear goal in sight and she knew the best ways to achieve those goals. As a mother caring for her children, she deals with projects that are not clearly defined. There is often no logical beginning or end to the tasks that need to be done. She cleans a room only to have it overturned a few minutes later. She cooks a meal that the children refuse to eat. She goes for weeks, months, years without a full night's sleep, waking to feed, change, and treat illnesses. For all of her work, there is no large paycheck in her name. The shopping she does is no longer for her, but for her children. In choosing motherhood, she accepted an infinite responsibility to care for others, namely, her children. She left a world in which her ego-self was firmly established, and handsomely rewarded, for a world in which she necessarily, but willingly, puts others first.

This is a shift of monumental importance and impact. This shift from professional life to motherhood demonstrates a move out of the realm of the same, the everyday world dominated by the interests of the ego, and into the ethical relation of infinite responsibility to care for others. The movement of care is generated out of desire for the other's well-being rather than the needs of self-interested ego. The movement of desire for or toward the other is made with the dynamic energy that constitutes the face-to-face relationship that Levinas calls ethical. This movement has parallels in Plato's classic tale of the prisoner who finds the good through education, as well as in the central driving force of Christian life, which is love.

Desire for the Other as a
Movement out of Fullness

The most famous passage in Plato's *Republic* is known as the allegory of the cave. Plato uses this allegory to present his understanding of the Good, which for him is the highest ideal and the highest reality in the entire cosmos. The allegory begins with a group of prisoners chained in a dark cave. They are unable to move their limbs or turn their heads. They can only look straight ahead. In front of them is a high wall and behind them is a loft in front of a fire. The light from the fire projects shadows of puppets, that are moved in front of the fire, onto the large wall in front of the prisoners. Since the prisoners have never seen anything else in their entire lives, they believe the shadows are all there is to reality.

Plato believes that the ignorance of the prisoners is analogous to the state of mind that all human beings experience early in life. For parents trying to navigate through the land mines of child rearing the feeling of ignorance or inadequacy is not uncommon. For Plato, the way to overcome ignorance is education. What is striking in our society, given the emphasis that we place on various types of education, is the lack of interest we show in the education of young people regarding what is likely to be their most important task—parenting.

Like the learning process that most parents must go through, the educational process that Plato envisages for overcoming ignorance is difficult. This difficulty stems from the need to let go of old habits and old ways of thinking and trying to develop and understand new ones. It means leaving behind friends, family, and customs that are comfortable and familiar in order to explore the uncertainties of new ideas and unfamiliar paths. When these uncertainties concern a child's health, or education, or safety, we can easily feel overwhelmed.

For Plato, the process of education, if successful, leads one to an intellectual, rational comprehension of the Good. Knowledge of the Good is the highest wisdom, and thus, the highest aspiration, of the philosophical life. Plato describes the Good as analogous to the sun. Just as the eyes need the light of the sun to see the natural world, the soul needs the light of the Good to see the spiritual world. For Plato, the spiritual world of ideals is more permanent and more real than the ever-changing natural world.

After undergoing the arduous educational journey to achieve the highest wisdom available to the soul, one would imagine that the philosopher would rest content outside the dark walls of the cave. But Plato does not end the allegory there. Upon attaining a vision of the Good, the philosopher or person of wisdom is compelled to go back into the cave to share his wisdom with his old prison mates. Even though he knows before returning that he will not be well received, and may even be killed for bringing word of a completely different and superior reality, he must go back. But why must he go back? Why not just bask in the pleasures of his newfound wisdom?

Although Plato is often criticized for overemphasizing the intellectual dimension of experience, the allegory of the cave lends itself to an interpretation of wisdom that goes beyond the intellectual. For Plato, knowledge is virtue and virtue is knowledge. That is, if one really knows what the right thing to do is, he will do it. In Plato's view, when we fail to do the right thing, we just don't understand the situation well enough. As one leaves the cave of ignorance to gain sight of reality, which is the Good, it is not a mere intellectual exercise, like solving a crossword puzzle. To gain wisdom is to undergo a radical conversion. To know the Good is to become good. So the prisoner cannot stay outside the cave, because the nature of what he has come to understand compels him to go back. If he refused to go back, it would be an indication that he did not really know the Good. It is the nature of the Good to be shared. When one knows the Good, and becomes good, he must share the Good, because it cannot be contained. It overflows the individual. The Good increases as it is shared and diminishes if not shared.

For parents who have a healthy sense of self, the fullness of the Good is often the motivation for how they care for their children. Unlike Plato's philosopher, however, parents need to get to the Good at the beginning of their journey and not at the end. It is of little value to children if parents only realize the fullness of the Good as a source of motivation when their children are grown. Hence, parents probably need the benefits of philosophical wisdom.

This reading of the Good in Plato has deep similarities to the movement of desire in the ethical relation that Levinas uncovers. Unlike need, which

stimulates movement to satisfy a lack, desire, like Plato's Good, is a movement toward the other out of fullness. When a parent welcomes or cares for
her child out of the ethical obligation at the root of her being, she is not
seeking to satisfy something that she lacks. The movement of desire is a
movement for the sake of the other, with no expectation of receiving something in return. Like the prisoner who knows that he will likely be harmed
for sharing the Good, the movement ignited by desire is not concerned about
what is in it for the ego-self. In desiring the other's well-being, one expresses
a primordial dimension of one's higher self.

The Good, Desire, and Love

Plato's Good and Levinas's desire also share essential qualities with the central motivating force in the Christian understanding of human nature—love.
Thomas Merton, a Christian monk and mystic, opens his work *No Man Is an
Island* with a simple but profound meditation of the nature of love. His description of love could be interpreted as a commentary on Levinas's distinction between movement motivated by the needs of the ego and movement
motivated by desire in the ethical relation. Merton writes:

> There is a false and momentary happiness in self-satisfaction, but it always
> leads to sorrow because it narrows and deadens our spirit. True happiness is
> found in unselfish love, a love which increases in proportion as it is shared.
> There is no end to the sharing of love, and, therefore, the potential happiness
> of such love is without limit. Infinite sharing is the law of God's inner life. He
> has made sharing of ourselves the law of our own being, so that it is in loving
> others that we best love ourselves.[2]

The false and momentary happiness that Merton describes is the happiness that is sought by the ego-self in the realm of the same, or the realm of
economy. This is the result of movement or activity generated out of need.
True happiness is found when one shares love unselfishly, just as for Levinas
one's highest nature desires the well-being of the other in the ethical relation. Just as the prisoner in Plato's allegory of the cave cannot keep the Good
to himself, but is compelled to share it, Levinas's desire and Merton's love increase in proportion as they are given away. If one acts on the motivations
that arise out of the highest, most spiritual dimensions of human nature, the
resources of the Good, love, and desire are infinite.

Most of us never get all the way out of Plato's cave. The light of reality or
of the face of the other is too strong for our eyes, and we try to live content

with dimmer images generated by television and computer screens. Most of us spend so much time and energy trying to meet the challenges generated by the needs of the ego that we fail to see the face of the other, whether our children's, our friends', or a stranger's, as other. We tend to reduce the face of the other to a mere resource for our own benefit. This precludes the possibility of experiencing the infinite mystery of the other and the infinite responsibility that we have to care for the other. We are so forcefully bombarded by messages that happiness is found in satisfying the fleeting needs of the ego-self, that our ability to love selflessly is often severely compromised. Hence, we often find ourselves gasping for a breath of true happiness.

Yet, I think that many parents understand the difference between the real and the illusory in Plato, need and desire in Levinas, and false and true happiness in Merton. The challenge we face as parents is to deepen our understanding of these distinctions by allowing ourselves to be moved by the higher callings of the Good, desire, and love. This is what most parents want for themselves and their children. Some have the courage to make the necessary changes to be moved by the higher callings of human nature: callings that often come from their children.

In a world so focused on the ego-self, its freedom, and its rights, it is difficult to imagine one living up to the call of infinite responsibility for others, unless one is a witness to the work of good parents. Consistently, parents respond to the call of their children out of a desire for their well-being. Good parents do this not so that their children might bring them some honor or pride, or some other type of reward. Good parents provide and care for their children so that their children can become happy, self-sufficient human beings. Good parents understand Levinas's account of the movement of desire as a movement out of fullness. It is a movement toward and for the other, but it is a movement that is never consummated in union or completion. In moving toward the other we experience the other as infinite, and no matter how much of our responsibility we meet, there is always more. The infinity of the other, of the child, ensures that the parent and the child remain separate and independent, even in the most intensely loving relationship.

In choosing to write about Levinas to a lay audience, I have little doubt that parents will understand his idea of the ethical relation, even though many philosophers have great difficulty in understanding it. Parents live it. They see the trace of God in the face of their child. They are moved by the innocence and infinity of the child. They see the care of their child as the single most important task of their life. They know that the child cannot and should not be reduced to the parent's conception of what is good or bad, acceptable or unacceptable. They care for the child in a way that gives the child the resources to achieve the best life possible. Given that self-sacrifice that seems so natural to good parents, it is surprising to me that Levinas does not draw on the parent–child relationship more often to demonstrate the intricacies of the ethical relation.

But I emphasize that it is the *good* parents who understand and live the ethical relation. There are many well-intentioned parents who have a difficult time living a life of perpetual self-sacrifice. They have a difficult time overcoming movement motivated by lack and need in the realm of economy. For these parents, the needs of the ego-self have yet to be worked out, and these needs retain a devastating hold on their soul and on their relationship with their children. In such cases, children suffer and parents are unhappy.

Healthy parents understand that they must attend to their own emotional, psychological, spiritual, and physical needs, even though they are elements of the realm of the same, of self-interest, if they are to be capable of caring for their children in an appropriate way. In doing so, however, they understand that the ethical relation is primary and primordial. Their obligation toward their children is the context in which their other interests and concerns find meaning. Levinas presents the primordiality of the ethical relation as the universal human condition, not something we freely choose. For him, our obligation toward the other holds us hostage from the start.

While many philosophers doubt this claim, parents know it to be true regarding their relationship with their children. The parent–child relationship provides evidence that human beings, at the very core of their existence, do feel responsible for the well-being of others. In caring for their children, parents reveal what it means to move toward the other out of the fullness of desire. Parents who find the challenge of expanding such desire beyond their immediate family difficult should be reassured that the loving desire they have for their children is worthy of praise and honor. They should realize that in caring for their child they are responding to the highest calling of human life. In the face of the child is the infinite or trace of God. The face calls for our infinite responsibility. We move toward the other out of the fullness of desire for the other's well-being. In this movement, we fulfill our human potential.

Given the magnitude of the ethical relation that Levinas describes, and the natural instincts of a parent to enact that relationship, the woman who chose to leave her successful career embodied the movement of our highest human calling. She understood that there was more to be done with her life than organizing numbers, books, and people. She didn't forget those skills or even leave them behind. She does the household finances. She researches and plans for her children's education. She remembers to bring medicines on vacation in case the children get sick. So her skills for organization serve her well as a parent. In fact, sometimes her talents make parenting a little more difficult for her, because of the inevitable frustration that ensues when her high standards for order and organization are not met. But over and above the frustrations, the headstrong battles with her children, and the occasional longing for the nicer car that she could buy if she were working profession-ally, she lives a life in which she is moved by the fullness of the Good, love, and desire for the well-being of her children. The enthusiasm for life that her children exude as a result is a marvel to observe. And I do every day, because she is the mother of my three children. She is my wife.

Notes

1. Kathleen Norris, *Amazing Grace: A Vocabulary of Faith* (New York: Riverhead, 1998), 150–51.

2. Thomas Merton, *No Man Is an Island* (New York: Harcourt, Brace, Jovanovich, 1955), 3.

EPILOGUE

~

The Evolving
Challenges of Parenting

It is difficult to be a good parent. Parents, and commentators on parenting, need to remember that the complexity of growing children and teenagers makes parenting an imprecise activity. No parent can fully know or understand the motivations, needs, doubts, fears, joys, weaknesses, or strengths of children. Nobody should expect them to. Every child, every parent, and the circumstances of every family are different. Therefore, there is no comprehensive manual to which parents can refer to find the exact technique or procedure for every situation. For this reason, the subtitle of this book refers to parenting as an art.

Like any art, parenting requires patience and practice, experimentation and confidence. It takes time and repetition to skillfully overcome the many obstacles on the way to proficiency. New approaches are tried; some work, some do not. But in each situation, parents are called on to be in control, to set the tone and the direction for their children to follow. As almost all parents know, however, it is difficult to always maintain control, to have fresh ideas and a clear vision of what needs to be accomplished. In our society, unfortunately, parenting seems to be getting even more difficult. As Cornell West and Sylvia Hewlet argue in *The War against Parents*, the social structures that traditionally supported healthy family life have shifted over the past thirty years. Parents are expected to do more for their children with less time and less money. With the demise of communities and neighborhoods in which children could roam freely and safely, parents are forced to schedule playtimes and transport their children to and fro. As

Kieran Bonner points out in *Power and Parenting*, unlike traditional family arrangements in which the nuclear family was surrounded and supported by an extended family, today's nuclear families are very often isolated and alone. As a result, parents are given complete power over their children, with nobody to offer correctives to the mistakes they inevitably make. Along with complete power comes complete responsibility. Parents alone are held accountable for how children develop and behave. For parents who cannot afford supplemental care and cannot get a break from the intensity of being with children constantly, it is difficult to sustain a healthy and nurturing family environment.

As I think back on my own childhood and the neighborhood in which I grew up, which is the same neighborhood I now live in, I see firsthand evidence of the detrimental shifts that have taken place. One of the most distinctive memories of my modest basketball career dates back to the summer of 1979. I was waiting around the sidelines of the courts where some of the best high school players in New York City came to play. I used to go there every day to watch, hoping and waiting for the day I would be asked to play. Between games I would go onto the court to shoot while the next team of five were getting organized to take on the team that had won the previous game. Although I had a decent reputation as a grammar school player, I was still at least two years younger than almost all of the other players. So I understood being overlooked, but I hung around waiting for the day things would change.

One afternoon the park began to fill with players, and the first two teams were being picked. It was down to the last player and I was still waiting and hoping. Bobby Cooper was the oldest of five brothers and six sisters and already out of high school. He was well known and respected among all of the people in the park. To my surprise and delight, he spoke up on my behalf, asking loud enough to be heard by everyone, "How is the kid going to make his high school team if you don't let him play?" I was chosen, and the team I played on held the court for the entire day, winning five or six games in a row until it got dark. From that day until I went away to play ball at college, I was always picked to be on a team in the park.

Neighborhoods like mine, which provided safe places for children to grow, play, and develop lifelong friendships, are almost all gone. From the age of twelve to the age of seventeen, I ran to the park six days a week to play ball. I ran because once the games started there were always fifteen or more people waiting to play, which meant waiting at least three games if you were on the last team. The park in which Bobby Cooper took a stand on my behalf is two short blocks from where I now live. I pass by the courts almost daily. Sadly, they are always empty. In my neighborhood there are more people, more families, and more children than when I was a child, but there is less of a community. While the basketball courts are empty, houses with day care are full. Mothers and fathers drop off their children between six and eight in the morning, and return to pick them up between six and eight in the evening. The women who run these day cares are well intentioned and hardworking, but there is only so much they can provide to eight, or ten, or more young children each day. Whereas my parents would open the door and tell me what time to be home, knowing that I would be late if I got into one extra game at the park, parents today are working long hours, hoping to get an extra hour of overtime. Whereas I learned to be a teenager by observing, listening to, and playing with teenagers, adolescents today master video games or wait to be driven to a friend's house to play.

My childhood wasn't ideal. Many of the teenagers were smoking dope and drinking kegs from Carvel cups after they played ball. We all began drinking too young. But Bobby Cooper wasn't interested in having me smoke dope. He was interested in having me become a better ball player. While my parents probably weren't aware of it at the time, they relied on people like Bobby Cooper to help raise me. They trusted in him because they trusted in the community, in families and friends, and in the activities around which the community revolved. But they could trust in the community because they were an integral part of it. They could comfortably raise a family of four on a union carpenter's wages supplemented with a few side jobs. This allowed them to be home when we needed them and even when we didn't.

The evidence that West and Hewlet give to demonstrate that our current political, social, and economic policies are failing families is demoralizing. The economic burdens in particular are pushing both parents into the workforce and keeping many single parents near the poverty line. We need to be aware of these systemic failures, and work wherever we can to reverse them. Most importantly, in thinking about becoming better parents—whether that means working for political and social change or developing a better understanding of our children—we need fresh and insightful perspectives to achieve improvement. These perspectives can best be found through alternative, philosophical ways of thinking. As long as the roar of mainstream media drives the ideas and interests of parents, change will continue to be for the worse.

The demise of community life, increasing economic burdens, and the ever-rising decibels of mainstream materialism are all increasing the challenges of parenting today. While the systemic failures pose obvious difficulties for those who are on the lower end of the economic scale, parental difficulties do not spare the wealthy. Those who have ample economic resources may not have the stresses of meeting monthly bill payments or finding time away from the children to be with adults. But they must carefully, thoughtfully navigate between the freedom available to them and their children's need to have them around. They must negotiate which values will be passed on to their children and who will pass those values on. It must be very tempting for parents who can afford full-time nannies to be with their children only in their easy moments. But it is out of the difficult times—the dirty diapers, the defiant stances, the headstrong negotiations, the hurt feelings, and the injured bodies—that deep and loving relationships grow and flourish. There is no substitute for the parental work these moments involve. Regardless of the economic, social, and cultural circumstances of a family, it is difficult to be a good parent.

As seventeenth-century philosopher Baruch Spinoza writes at the end of his classic work *The Ethics*, "All things excellent are as difficult as they are rare."[1] The art of parenting, when done well, influences the development of the most important legacy parents will leave to the world. But it is difficult to become an artful parent. Those parents who are successful stand out among us, along with their children. These parents are willing to step back from the frenetic pace and stress of everyday life to recapture a sense of wonder and engage in thoughtful contemplation. The contemplative mind opens new horizons of understanding, within which stressful situations are made small or even insignificant. For a healthy mind and a healthy perspective on family life, we need to supplement the practical mind with contemplation.

By opening ourselves to alternative modes of thought, we discover things that we already know about parenting but that often go unnoticed under the diversions and concerns of everyday life. Every human being is the beneficiary of generations of cultural and genetic wisdom that has been refined over the course of human history. Through thoughtful reflection, we can cultivate this inherited wisdom into what Aristotle called practical wisdom. The person of practical wisdom clarifies for herself and for her children what we aspire to become as human beings. We need to know what we honestly believe is the best life for our children and for ourselves. Without serious reflection on this issue, we are likely to be led astray. If we are led astray, we will prove to be ineffective guides for our children.

The self-reflection that is required to clarify our highest aspirations and the values we want to live by will often force us to confront uncomfortable, even painful, memories harbored deep within the psyche. Many parents carry emotional and psychological wounds from their own childhood. But just as it is necessary that good parents face up to the difficult situations that involve their children, it is equally essential that they face up to the difficulties they have endured in their own lives. Unless these wounds are sorted out and dealt with honestly, they are likely to negatively affect the abilities of a parent to love and nurture her children.

Parents need to be the adults in their relationships with their children. Parents need to be compassionate, understanding, and caring. To do so they must develop capacities for listening and live, to the best of their abilities, a life of virtue. But parents must also be confident and firm as their children's teachers. As children follow their natural and necessary paths of separation and individuation, they are looking to parents not only for encouragement but also for appropriate boundaries to guide them. Children need to know the difference between right and wrong. They learn this primarily by imitating the adults they admire, beginning with their parents. But they also need to know that the world is not going to appease their every whim. As they resist parental authority and forge their own identity, parents must provide sensible, intelligent, and intelligible boundaries within which their development can take place. This will often lead to rifts between parents and children, but when the motivation is to help the child reach her potential as a human being, the prevailing force of parental love usually overcomes these rifts. In this parents can be confident.

The fact that modern society is forcing parents to become ever more self-reliant has its negative consequences. But in these increasingly demanding times, reflective and resourceful parents will find artful ways to nurture and guide their children. Different times provide different challenges and different resources for parents to meet those challenges. But there has always been a need for parents to stand above all others in the eyes of their children and in their own eyes. That is, artful parents have always been called to develop a strong sense of independence and self-reliance. To be self-reliant is to have the insight to know what endures and what does not, regardless of the values and the messages of the mainstream. It entails having the wisdom to search for happiness and peace in what endures, in what is central to the human enterprise, and to look askance at imposters of happiness and peace. Ralph Waldo Emerson, at the end of his classic essay *Self-Reliance*, powerfully captures the central tenet of this wisdom. He writes:

"A political victory, a rise of rents, the recovery of your sick or the return of your absent friend, or some other favorable event raises your spirits, and you think good days are preparing for you. Do not believe it. Nothing can bring you peace but yourself. Nothing can bring you peace but the triumph of principles."[2] Nothing can bring a parent, a family, or a child peace but the triumph of principles.

Notes

1. Baruch Spinoza, *The Ethics and Selected Letters*, trans. Samuel Shirley (Indianapolis: Hackett, 1982), 225.

2. Ralph Waldo Emerson, "Self-Reliance," in *Selected Essays* (New York: Penguin, 1982), 203.

Bibliography

Abram, David. *The Spell of the Sensuous*. New York: Vintage, 1996.

Aristotle. *The Basic Works of Aristotle*. Ed. Richard McKeon. New York: Random House, 1968.

Barbe, Nigel. *Why Parents Matter: Parental Investment and Child Outcomes*. Westport, Conn.: Bergin and Garvey, 2000.

Berry, Thomas. *The Dream of the Earth*. San Francisco: Sierra, 1988.

Bonner, Kieran. *Power and Parenting: A Hermeneutic of the Human Condition*. New York: St. Martin's, 1998.

Coles, Robert. *The Moral Intelligence of Children*. New York: Random House, 1997.

Descartes, Rene. *Discourse on Method and Meditations on First Philosophy*. New York: Hackett, 1980.

Eliot, T. S. *The Four Quartets*. New York: Harcourt, Brace, Jovanovich, 1971.

Emerson, Ralph Waldo. *Selected Essays*. New York: Penguin, 1982.

Erikson, Erik. *Identity and the Life Cycle*. New York: Norton, 1980.

Faber, Adele, and Elaine Mazlish. *How to Talk So Your Kids Will Listen and Listen So Your Kids Will Talk*. New York: Avon, 1999.

———. *Siblings without Rilvary: How to Help Your Children Live Together So You Can Live Too*. New York: Avon, 1998.

Golombok, Susan. *Parenting: What Really Counts?* London: Routledge, 2000.

Gottleib, Roger. *Joining Hands: Politics and Religion Together for Social Change*. Boulder, Colo.: Westview, 2002.

Hannush, Mufid J. *Becoming Good Parents: An Existential Journey*. Albany: State University of New York Press, 2002.

Heaney, Seamus. *Death of a Naturalist*. Boston: Faber and Faber, 1966.

Heidegger, Martin. *Basic Writings*. Trans. David Krell. New York: Harper Collins, 1993.

———. *Being and Time*. Trans. John Macquarrie and Edward Robinson. New York: Harper and Row, 1962.

Hewlet, Sylvia, and Cornell West. *The War against Parents: What We Can Do for America's Beleaguered Moms and Dads*. New York: Houghton Mifflin, 1998.

Keen, Sam. *Apology for Wonder*. New York: Harper Collins, 1980.

Kittay, Eva F. *Love's Labor: Essays on Women, Equality, and Dependency*. Boston: Routledge, 1998.

Levin, David Michael. *The Body's Recollection of Being*. Boston: Routledge and Kegan, 1985.

———. *The Listening Self*. Boston: Routledge, 1989.

———. *The Opening of Vision*. Boston: Routledge, 1988.

Levinas, Emmanuel. *Totality and Infinity*. Trans. Alphonso Lingis. Pittsburgh: Duquesne University Press, 1984.

Merleau-Ponty, M. *The Phenomenology of Perception*. Trans. Colin Smith. Atlantic Heights, N.J.: Humanities, 1992.

———. *The Visible and the Invisible*. Trans. Alphonso Lingis. Evanston, Ill.: Northwestern University Press, 1984.

Merton, Thomas. *No Man Is an Island*. New York: Harcourt, Brace, Jovanovich, 1955.

Miller, Alice. *The Drama of the Gifted Child: The Search for the True Self*. New York: Basic, 1997.

Needleman, Jacob. *The Heart of Philosophy*. New York: Harper, 1986.

———. *Money and the Meaning of Life*. New York: Doubleday, 1984.

Norris, Kathleen. *Amazing Grace: A Vocabulary of Faith*. New York: Riverhead, 1998.

Pearce, Joseph. *Magical Child*. New York: Plume, 1977.

Peck, M. Scott. *The Road Less Traveled: A New Psychology of Love, Traditional Values, and Spiritual Growth*. New York: Simon and Schuster, 1978.

Peirce, Charles S. *Philosophical Writings of Peirce*. Ed. Justus Buchler. New York: Dover, 1955.

Plato. *Collected Works of Plato*. Ed. Edith Hamilton and Huntington Cairns. Princeton, N.J.: Princeton University Press, 1961.

———. *Dialogues of Plato*. Trans. W. H. D. Rouse. New York: Mentor, 1984.

Rogers, Carl. *On Becoming a Person: A Therapist's View of Psychotherapy*. New York, Houghton Mifflin, 1995.

Ruddick, Sara. *Maternal Thinking: Toward a Politics of Peace*. Boston: Beacon, 1995.

Schumacher, E. F. *Small Is Beautiful: Economics As If People Mattered*. New York: Harper and Row, 1989.

Schupak, Sonna. *Children as Teachers*. New York: Sarah Lawrence College Press, forthcoming.

Soulter, Aletha. *Helping Your Children to Flourish*. Goleta, Calif.: Shining Star, 1994.

Spinoza, Baruch. *The Ethics and Selected Letters*. Trans. Samuel Shirley. Indianapolis: Hackett, 1982.

Swimme, Brian. *The Universe Is a Green Dragon*. Santa Fe, N. Mex.: Bear, 1984.

Tillich, Paul. *The Courage to Be*. New Haven, Conn.: Yale University Press, 1952.

Tolstoy, Leo. *The Death of Ivan Ilych and Other Stories*. New York: Penguin, 1960.

Whitman, Walt. *Leaves of Grass*. New York: Barnes and Noble, 1993.

Winnicott, Donald. *Playing and Reality*. London: Routledge, 1980.

Index

~

About the Author

Seamus Carey holds a Ph.D. in philosophy and teaches at Manhattan College in Riverdale, New York. He has published several articles and reviews in the areas of continental and environmental philosophy. Between writing projects, Dr. Carey builds and restores residential housing. He lives in New York with his wife and three children.